McGraw-Hill's
Quick and Easy
Medical Spanish

A HANDS-ON GUIDE TO SPANISH BASICS

CLAUDIA KECHKIAN

New York   Chicago   San Francisco   Lisbon   London   Madrid   Mexico City
Milan   New Delhi   San Juan   Seoul   Singapore   Sydney   Toronto

1 2 3 4 5 6 7 8 9 0   VLP/VLP   0 9 8 7 6 5

ISBN 0-07-145964-2 (book and CD package)
ISBN 0-07-145965-0 (book only)

Library of Congress Control Number 2005927553

McGraw-Hill books are available at special quantity discounts to use as premiums and sales promotions, or for use in corporate training programs. For more information, please write to the Director of Special Sales, Professional Publishing, McGraw-Hill, Two Penn Plaza, New York, NY 10121-2298. Or contact your local bookstore.

All situations are fictitious. All names, addresses, telephone numbers, and medical situations are used for instructional purposes only.

This book is printed on acid-free paper.

Contents

Acknowledgments

I want to thank all my students along my twenty-year language teaching career, through whom I learned and experienced that teaching and learning a language can be serious, effective, and fun, all together at the same time. Thank you for so many years of joy, happiness, and hard but rewarding work!

Special thanks to each and all of my students at the Physician Assistant Program, Barry University School of Graduate Medical Sciences, Miami Shores, Florida, for your positive attitudes, enthusiasm, and great work in my Medical Spanish classes. I truly appreciate the Barry University community!

Thanks to all of the editors for the work we shared as a real team throughout the editing process, and to the designers for a great job. Thank you, also, to the publisher for opening the doors of this book to all its potential readers.

To my parents, all my family, and friends in Argentina and the United States. I am thankful to you and hope each of you knows how much I treasure your love, friendship, and support.

To my husband and daughters. Thank you for your friendly company and your encouragement! I could have never written this book without your consistent support along the way. I love you!

Introduction

McGraw-Hill's Quick and Easy Medical Spanish is a Spanish language program tailored to your needs as a health care professional to communicate with your Spanish-speaking patients.

The contents of the book have been carefully selected and planned so that the language is acquired gradually and naturally. All the situations presented are related to common situations that take place in a hospital or physician's office. Each lesson presents vocabulary relevant to the situation at hand, opening the door to new and different situations that you will gradually add to your language experience.

You will incorporate, use, and recycle the Spanish language at every moment through a lively integration of the four language skills: listening, speaking, reading, and writing. This will allow you to start using the language right from the very first chapter, gradually enlarging your communication skills through various activities and through the continuous incorporation of medical terms and vocabulary.

The book begins with an overview of Spanish pronunciation and grammar, followed by eleven chapters organized in six steps, plus three appendices: Appendix 1, Medical Specialties, focusing on areas of vocabulary; Appendix 2, Verb References, focusing on the use of verbs and conjugation guidelines; and Appendix 3, Answer Key, which gives the answers to the dialog comprehension sections and written exercises in each chapter. There are summary Self-Check Exercises after Chapters 5 and 10.

Everything is here for you, so enjoy your language-learning experience, and do your best to break down your present language barriers! It's easier than you may think! Just go ahead, trust yourself, and try to incorporate the language little by little into your everyday life. Each time you try you will certainly have a different and more positive perception, and hopefully you will soon experience the benefits of speaking your patient's language.

How to Use This Book

The working methodology in this book has been organized in six steps, which will guide your work throughout the learning process. This organization is based on the Kechkian Language in Action approach, which prioritizes the integration of the four language skills—listening, speaking, reading, and writing—and will take you gradually from language exposure and practice to language production.

You will first listen to a dialog and go through meaningful repetition and practice of the target language structures and vocabulary, presented both in Spanish and English. This bilingual presentation will make the repetition and practice process a fast and effective way to help you incorporate the new vocabulary and structures, by facilitating a quick process of language structure comparison, and the association of the new words with their exact meaning by means of their actual equivalents. Then, through the steps that follow, you will make sure you understand all the grammatical aspects necessary to build the language on solid ground, practice all the key structures through guided speaking exercises, use the language that starts to become familiar to you in guided written exercises, and get to the final step—the role-playing exercise, through which you will actually produce the language. This role-playing activity will become the most tangible evidence that the language has been and is being acquired, and will open a door that will enable you to use the language in new situations.

Step 1: Dialog with General Comprehension Questions

 With the CD

- Listen to the dialog, which presents the new language in a meaningful context. At this point, you only need to get a general context and a global comprehension. So take your time, and you will be ready to understand the complete dialog shortly!

With Your Workbook

- Read while you listen to the dialog and try to figure out the meaning of words that sound similar to English words. Context and intonation may guide you too.

- Check your comprehension by choosing the correct options in the Dialog Comprehension section. You will be addressed either in English or in Spanish at this point, depending on whether the question or statement is intended to elicit just comprehension or both comprehension and production from your part. Please, address these in the same language they are presented. You can check your answers in the Answer Key.

Step 2: Vocabulary Practice

With the CD

- You will be introduced to all the new language items, which you will understand through translation and incorporate through meaningful repetition.

- Practice aloud pronunciation and intonation.

- Listen carefully, check understanding, and get ready to repeat or even imitate the audio when it is your turn!

With Your Workbook

- Take advantage of the alphabetical order of the words in English.

- Make sure you understand each new item.

- Read the Spanish equivalents aloud. This is also a good time to check pronunciation with the audio, while you reinforce your reading skills.

- When in doubt about how to read a word, you can check the pronunciation guidelines by referring to the Spanish Pronunciation and Grammar Basics section that follows this section.

Step 3: Grammar in Use

With Your Workbook

- Review the grammatical structure of the Spanish language and compare it with the English structure.

- Do not worry if you find you are getting lost somewhere. Just use what you feel is helpful.

- Read the information, understand it, associate it, and go ahead to the next step!

Step 4: Speaking Exercises

With the CD

- Listen to the dialog presented in each chapter once again. You will notice how much more you will understand this time! If there is still a word you cannot get, don't hesitate to go to a dictionary. By this point, you are ready to have a complete comprehension of it.

- Be active! Interact with the CD as required. The prompts will guide you to take part in a variety of situations. The only way to start speaking is just by... practicing!

With Your Workbook

- Read the dialog while you try to change the information provided.

- You can follow the prompts in your book to practice without the CD.

- You may want to practice before interacting with the audio, to get the language at the tip of your tongue!

- Or you also can practice after interacting with the audio, to improve your fluency and accuracy.

Step 5: Written Exercises

With Your Workbook

- At this point you are ready to put in writing all the language you have been acquiring and practicing throughout the previous steps. Remember that once you become familiar with the alphabet and the sounds, you write as you speak and as you hear!

- Self-correct your answers with the Answer Key at the end of your book, and refer back to the corresponding section of your book when necessary.

Step 6: Role-Playing Exercise

With the CD

- Listen to the prompts on the CD and interact with the narrator as if you were in a real situation.

- Try to imagine yourself in the situation, and place the dialog in the given context.

- Enjoy and take advantage of the role-playing exercise, since it represents the closest approximation to real conversation.

With Your Workbook

- This section also lets you practice without the CD, using the prompts in your book.

- You can keep practicing the dialogs both before and after interacting with the audio to achieve as much fluency as you can!

Spanish Pronunciation and Grammar Basics

 Before starting to learn the Spanish language, it is important to take some sounds into consideration. Repeat the words below to practice the sounds; then read each complete sentence, focusing on its target letter.

Las vocales *The Vowels*

Spanish vowels are pronounced differently from English. This is a key to a correct pronunciation in Spanish. Once we identify the vowel sounds we are almost ready to read correctly, as in Spanish words are pronounced and read exactly as they are written.

A   is pronounced /**ah**/. There is only one pronunciation for *a* in Spanish; it is like a neutral *a,* a mixture of the sounds in "map" and "car."

   Amanda   **amar** (love)   **las** (the)   **manzanas** (apples)   **asadas** (baked)

   Amanda ama las manzanas asadas.
   Amanda loves baked apples.

E   is pronounced /**eh**/, as in "pet," "net," "let."

   Este (this)   **es** (is)   **el** (the)   **bebé** (baby)   **de** (of)   **Belén**

   Este es el bebé de Belén.
   This is Belén's baby.

I   is pronounced /**ee**/. There is only one pronunciation of *i.* Again it is neutral. It is not as short as in "lip," and not as long as in "deep."

   Lis   **y** (and)   **Lilí**   **visitar** (visit)   **París** (Paris)

   Lis y Lilí visitan París.
   Lis and Lilí visit Paris.

   Note: *Y* in isolation means "and," and it is pronounced /**ee**/.

O   is pronounced /**oh**/, as in "dog," "mop."

   Rodolfo   **comer** (eat)   **postre** (dessert)   **coco** (coconut)

   Rodolfo comió postre de coco.
   Rodolfo ate coconut cake.

U   is pronounced /**oo**/, as in "moon," "tuna."

   Lulú   **gustar** (like)   **luz** (light)   **luna** (moon)

   A Lulú le gusta la luz de la luna.
   Lulú likes the moonlight.

Las consonantes *The Consonants*

A few consonants and syllables should be taken into consideration to manage good pronunciation. You will see how you will get used to these sounds as you go along!

G   has two pronunciations:
/**g**/ as in "gate"

Greta   **gustar** (like)   **golf** (golf)

A Greta le gusta el golf.
Greta likes golf.

/**h**/ or strong /**h**/ as in "hot" **when followed** by *e* or *i.*

Gerardo   **agencias** (agencies)   **Ginebra** (Geneva)

Gerardo tiene agencias en Ginebra.
Gerardo has agencies in Geneva.

In the syllables *gue* and *gui* the *u* is silent. These combinations are pronounced /**ge**/ as in "target" and /**gi**/ as in "give." For example: **guía** (guide), **manguera** (hose).
In the syllables *güe* and *güi* the dots on the *u (diéresis)* show that the *u* is pronounced. There are very few words with these syllables, though. For example: **lingüística** (linguistics), **paragüería** (umbrella shop).

H   is silent, not pronounced at all.

Hugo   **hospital** (hospital)   **hipertensión** (hypertension)

Hugo está en el hospital con hipertensión.
Hugo is in the hospital with hypertension.

J   is pronounced like a very strong guttural *h,* stronger than the *h* in "hot."

Juan Jiménez   **viajar** (travel)   **Japón** (Japan)   **julio** (July)

Juan Jiménez viajó a Japón en julio.
Juan Jiménez traveled to Japan in July.

The pronunciation of *j* will vary among speakers from different countries. People from Spain and Argentina tend to pronounce it quite strongly.

Ñ   is pronounced /**ny**/, as in "bunion," "union."

señor (mister)   **Ordóñez**   **baño** (restroom)

El señor Ordóñez está en el baño.
Mr. Ordóñez is in the bathroom.

Q   is pronounced /k/, and it appears in the syllables *que* and *qui,* where the *u* is silent.

    Enrique Quiroga   **quesos** (cheese)   **exquisitos** (exquisite)

    Enrique Quiroga come quesos exquisitos.
    Enrique Quiroga eats exquisite (types of) cheese.

LL and **Y** are pronounced /y/, as in "papaya."

    millas (miles)   **llegar** (arrive)   **playa** (beach)

    Hay dos millas para llegar a la playa.
    It's two miles to get to the beach.

R   as an initial letter and double *r* is strong and rolled.

    Rosa   **perro** (dog)   **marrón** (brown)

    Rosa tiene un perro marrón.
    Rosa has a brown dog.

Stress

The stress in Spanish falls on the final syllable when the word ends in a consonant (except *n* and *s*) or if it ends in *y.*

    For example: *prosperidad* (prosperity), *oportunidad* (opportunity), *universidad* (university), *epidural* (epidural), *indicador* (indicator), *Uruguay.*

    When a word ends in a vowel, *n* or *s*, the stress will fall on the syllable preceding the last.

    For example: *intestino* (intestine), *cultivo* (culture), *ejercicio* (exercise), *paciente* (patient), *lumen* (lumen), *micosis* (mycosis).

Accent

An accent mark is used on vowels (*á, é, í, ó, ú*) to note a stressed syllable that does not follow the typical pattern.

    For example: *bebé* (baby), *lápiz* (pencil), *genético* (genetic), *anatomía* (anatomy), *hipertensión* (hypertension), *intoxicación* (intoxication).

    All question words take an accent:

        ¿Qué...? (What...?)
        For example: **¿Qué hora es?** (What time is it?)

        ¿Cuál...? (What...?/Which...?)
        For example: **¿Cuál es su nacionalidad?** (What is your nationality?)

        ¿Dónde...? (Where...?)
        For example: **¿De dónde es usted?** (Where are you from?)

        ¿Cómo...? (How...?)
        For example: **¿Cómo está el paciente?** (How is the patient?)

Verbs

All verbs in the infinitive form are easy to recognize in Spanish; they end in *-ar, -er,* or *-ir.* For example: *estudiar* (to study), *comer* (to eat), *partir* (to leave, to depart).

All regular verbs will follow their conjugation patterns according to these endings, while the conjugation of regular verbs will vary, and will have to be learned simply by using them.

You will find more on regular and irregular verbs in Appendix 2, Verb References, on page 137.

Cognates

There are a lot of cognate words in Spanish and English. These are words that are very similar in both languages, because they have the same origin and root. We find plenty of them in the medical field.

Let's see if you can identify the meaning of the following cognate verbs: *aceptar, admitir, analizar, autorizar, calmar, comunicar, contaminar, decidir, depender, desinfectar, examinar, fracturar, informar, interpretar, mantener, nutrir, observar, operar, preparar, progresar, recomendar, referir, sufrir, transmitir, usar, visitar, vomitar.*

We also find many cognate nouns and adjectives in the medical field. Let's see if you can identify the following words and associate them with their English counterparts: *abdomen, alergia, análisis, antiinflamatorio, biopsia, cáncer, dermatólogo, diabetes, enfisema, flexible, gastroenterólogo, genético, hepatitis, hereditario, hipertensión, imagen, inflamación, laringitis, maternidad, nutrición, órganos, osteoporosis, penicilina, proctólogo, respiratorio, radiología, rayos X, sinusitis, solución, transplante, tuberculosis, urólogo, vasectomía, vómito, xenofobia.*

Gender and Number

One of the most difficult things to handle when learning Spanish is probably the agreement between gender and number. Articles, nouns, and adjectives <u>all</u> agree in gender and number, plus verbs are also affected by number. For example:

La niña es alta.	The girl is tall.
Las niñas son altas.	The girls are tall.
El enfermero es muy bueno.	The (male) nurse is very good.
Los enfermeros son muy buenos.	The nurses are very good.
Tengo dolor en el pie izquierdo.	I have pain in the left foot.
Tengo dolor en la cadera derecha.	I have pain in the right hip.

Notice also the word order in the last two examples. Adjectives follow the noun they refer to.

The most important thing to consider here is that it is not necessary to handle gender and number perfectly, as communication does not depend merely on the perfect use of the language. Take your time, practice! Your language skills will gradually become more accurate. Always take into account that your priority is communication.

Chapter 1

Presentaciones

Introductions

In this chapter you will learn how to greet people and introduce yourself. You will also learn to recognize certain cultural aspects of these situations.

Dialog: Soy el doctor Valle

I Am Doctor Valle

 El doctor Valle y la doctora Robinson trabajan en el mismo hospital.
Dr. Valle and Dr. Robinson work in the same hospital.

Doctor Valle:	**Buenos días.**
Doctora Robinson:	**Buenos días.**
Doctor Valle:	**Soy el doctor Carlos Valle.**
Doctora Robinson:	**Soy la doctora Janet Robinson.**
Doctor Valle:	**Mucho gusto.**
Doctora Robinson:	**Un placer.**

Dialog Comprehension

Test your comprehension of the dialog by checking the correct options.

Do you think doctors Valle and Robinson:
already know each other? ☐
are meeting for the first time? ☐

Do you think they are:
shaking hands? ☐
just looking at each other? ☐

 ### Vocabulary Practice

In this section you will find words and phrases necessary to greet people and introduce yourself.

Saludos *Greetings*

Buenos días	Good morning
Buenas tardes	Good afternoon
Buenas noches	Good evening; good night

Presentándose *Introducing Yourself*

Soy   I am

If you are male:

Soy el doctor Carlos Valle.	I am (the) doctor Carlos Valle.
asistente médico Juan López	medical assistant Juan López
enfermero Manuel Díaz	nurse Manuel Díaz
paciente Raúl Gómez	patient Raúl Gómez
asociado médico John Mirás	physician assistant John Mirás
estudiante Imanol Pérez	student Imanol Pérez
alumno David Fuentes	student David Fuentes

If you are female:

Soy la doctora Janet Robinson.	I am (the) doctor Janet Robinson.
asistente médico María Bueno	medical assistant María Bueno
enfermera Manuela Rodríguez	nurse Manuela Rodríguez
paciente Teresa García	patient Teresa García
asociado médico Julia Benítez	physician assistant Julia Benítez
estudiante Sofía Fonte	student Sofía Fonte
alumna Sandra Villa	student Sandra Villa
Mucho gusto.	Nice to meet you.
Un placer.	A pleasure.

Grammar in Use

The Difference Between *Buenas* and *Buenos*

We say *Buenos días,* but *Buenas tardes* and *Buenas noches,* because adjectives in Spanish are affected both by number and by gender. Thus the masculine noun *días* (days) is accompanied by the adjective in its masculine form, *buenos;* and the feminine nouns *tardes* (afternoons) and *noches* (evenings, nights) are accompanied by the adjective in the feminine form, *buenas.*

Definite Articles

la, el   the

La and *el* are definite articles. They stand for the English word "the." *La* is the feminine form, and *el* is the masculine form. By using the definite article when introducing yourself, you are distinguishing yourself from a group of people that may have the same profession or role as you at the same place; you are being specific about who you are.

For example, if you just want to say, "I am a nurse," you only need to say *Soy enfermera.* However, if you want to introduce yourself and say, "I am nurse Stevens," you will say *Soy la enfermera Stevens,* since you are defining who you are.

No definite article is used when you introduce yourself by only saying your name. For example, if you want to say, "I am Mary Grant," you will say *Soy María Grant.*

Feminine, Masculine, and One-form Health Care Professions

Feminine form nouns generally end in *a: profesora, doctora, alumna, enfermera.*

Masculine form nouns generally end in *r* or *o: profesor, doctor, alumno, enfermero.* There are also **one-form nouns,** used both for masculine and feminine. They have inherent gender, which is shown by other words accompanying the noun, such as the article. Within this category we find a group of nouns that end in *-ante* or *-ente: estudiante, asistente, paciente.* Thus, *la estudiante* (the female student), *el estudiante* (the male student); *la asistente* (the female assistant), *el asistente* (the male assistant); *la paciente* (the female patient), *el paciente* (the male patient). We also find plenty of one-form health care professions ending in *-ista,* such as *anestesista* (anesthetist), *especialista* (specialist), *psicoanalista* (psychoanalyst), *oculista* (oculist), *optometrista* (optometrist), *ortodoncista* (orthodontist), *nutricionista* (nutritionist), *dietista* (dietician); and a group of professions that end in *-tra: pediatra* (pediatrician), *psiquiatra* (psychiatrist), *podiatra* (podiatrist), *obstetra* (obstetrician). Gender is then shown by the article *el* when referring to a male professional, and by the article *la* when referring to a female one.

The professions *asistente médico* and *asociado médico* also remain unchanged for masculine or feminine gender. It will be meaningful to state the difference between these two terms, which is simple. *Un asistente médico* is a medical assistant. A medical assistant provides administrative, clerical, or technical support to the physician. *Un asociado médico* is a physician assistant. A physician assistant practices medicine as a partner (*asociado*) to the physician, as a team, and under the physician's supervision. The term *asociado médico* is the official title in Spanish for "physician assistant" adopted by the American Academy of Physician Assistants.

Verbs

ser	to be
soy (first person singular)	I am

For example:

(Yo) <u>Soy</u> el doctor Valle.	<u>I am</u> (the) doctor Valle.
(Yo) <u>Soy</u> la enfermera Díaz.	<u>I am</u> (the) nurse Díaz.

Notice that we use *Soy...* in all cases when introducing ourselves, since the subject *yo* ("I") can be omitted, as it is already shown in the verb conjugation.

Notice the abbreviations *Dra.* for *doctora,* and *Dr.* for *doctor.*

Speaking Exercises

1. Listen to the dialog **"Soy el Dr. Valle"** again (CD track 2). You will notice it sounds very familiar to you this time! Then go to page 1 and practice reading the dialog, changing the information provided for the introductions.

2. How would you greet someone in the following situations according to the time of day?

    For example:

    At 3 P.M. you would say *¡Buenas tardes!*

    What would you say at:

8:00 A.M.	5:00 P.M.
10:00 P.M.	9:00 P.M.
11:00 A.M.	2:00 P.M.

3. Imagine you are at a hospital, on your first day of work as a nurse. Introduce yourself to your coworkers. Remember to say *Soy la enfermera...* if you are female and *Soy el enfermero...* if you are male. You can also do this exercise without the CD, following the prompts below:

    With coworker 1:

    Buenos días. Soy la Dra. López.

    ¡————————! ————————————.

    Mucho gusto.

    ————————————————.

    With coworker 2:

    Buenas tardes. Soy el anestesista Martínez.

    ¡————————! ————————————.

    Mucho gusto.

    ————————————————.

    With coworker 3:

    Buenas noches. Soy el asociado médico Mare.

    ¡————————! ————————————.

    Mucho gusto.

    ————————————————.

4. Now take part in the following dialog, introducing yourself as you would in real life. If none of the vocabulary in this chapter applies to your profession, look up the words you need in a dictionary, or just say your name.

    Buenas tardes.

    ¡————————————————!

Soy el Dr. Joaquín Pereyra.

_____

Mucho gusto.

_____

5. Informal introductions. Observe the following example and introduce yourself.

   A: **¡Hola! Soy Juan Ríos.**

   B: **¡Hola! Soy Mariela Fuente.**

   It's your turn now!

   A: **¡Hola! Soy Pablo Canteros.**

   B: _____

Written Exercises

1. Complete the following dialog between Dr. Fernández and patient Vásquez. They are introducing themselves.

   Dr. F: **¡Buenos días!**

   PV: (a) ¡_____!

   Dr. F: **Soy el Doctor Joaquín Fernández.**

   PV: (b) _____ **Emilio Vásquez.**

   Dr. F: **Mucho gusto.**

   PV: (c) _____.

2. Look at the names and professions below. Then think of how they would introduce themselves to their patients, and write your answers.

   Example:
   Juana Granados, nutricionista.
   Soy la nutricionista Juana Granados, mucho gusto.

   Beatriz Nuñez, enfermera.

   (a) _____

Pedro Bolaños, asociado médico.

(b) _____

Luis Pedras, anestesista.

(c) _____

3. Think of a situation in which you and a patient are introducing yourselves; then write the dialog.

_____

_____

_____

_____

_____

_____

Role-Playing Exercise

Presentándose *Introducing Yourself*

In the following situation you are a health care professional working in a hospital. You have to introduce yourself to your Spanish-speaking patient Raúl Baloco, who is there waiting for you. Play the CD track (5) and interact with him. Go ahead! You start the dialog! It's 9:00 P.M. Greet your patient and introduce yourself. You can also practice this activity without the CD, following the prompts below.

You: (greet your patient and introduce yourself)
Patient: **Buenas noches, soy el paciente Raúl Baloco, mucho gusto.**
You: (reply)

Cultural Information

In the doctor-patient relationship, as well as in many other situations, a firm handshake and eye contact are highly appropriate. A smile can also make a difference, providing the patient with extra support that will certainly be appreciated. The physician will not only represent someone who provides professional advice and service, but also someone who provides support and confidence.

In regard to names and last names, keep in mind that it is very common to find a married woman still using her maiden name, especially in documents and cards. When asked for her last name, she will usually make reference to both, or will say, for example: *García Martínez: García es mi apellido de soltera* (my maiden name), *y Martínez de casada* (married name), meaning, "García is my maiden name, and Martínez my married name." It is also very common to find both father and son with the same first name, which passes from generation to generation. This is often seen in families of Mexican origin.

Chapter 2

Entrevistando a un nuevo paciente

Interviewing a New Patient

In this chapter you will learn to exchange personal information: name, country or city of origin, nationality, occupation, place of work, and length of time living in a city or country. You will learn to take care of your patient's complaint, be introduced to some parts of the body, and learn how to inform your patient about the most common tests or exams. You will also find out about certain cultural aspects of the doctor-patient relationship.

Dialog: Primera visita al médico

First Visit to the Doctor

El paciente Pedro López visita el consultorio del Dr. Milton por primera vez.
Patient Pedro López visits Dr. Milton's office for the first time.

Dr. Milton:	**Good morning!**
Paciente López:	**Good morning! Sorry doctor, do you speak Spanish? ¿Habla español?**
Dr. Milton:	**Un poco.**
Paciente López:	**¡Buenos días!**
Dr. Milton:	**¿De dónde es usted?**
Paciente López:	**Soy de Venezuela.**
Dr. Milton:	**¿Cuánto tiempo hace que está aquí?**
Paciente López:	**Hace dos meses.**
Dr. Milton:	**¿Cuál es su nombre?**
Paciente López:	**Pedro...Pedro López.**
Dr. Milton:	**Bien, Pedro. ¿Cuál es el motivo de su consulta?**
Paciente López:	**Tengo dolores de cabeza muy frecuentes.**
Dr. Milton:	**Y ¿cuál es su ocupación?**
Paciente López:	**Soy empleado. Trabajo en un supermercado.**
Dr. Milton:	**Bien, vamos a hacer un chequeo general.**

Dialog Comprehension

Test your comprehension of the dialog by checking the correct options below.

El paciente es:

Raúl González	☐
Pedro López	☐
Susana Díaz	☐

The patient is from:

Brazil	☐
Panama	☐
Venezuela	☐

Where does the patient say he works?

in a supermarket?	☐
in a bank?	☐
in a restaurant?	☐

 Vocabulary Practice

In this section, you'll find words and phrases necessary to start communicating with your patient.

País/ciudad de origen *Country/City of Origin*

¿Dónde?	Where?
¿De <u>dónde</u> es <u>usted</u>?	<u>Where</u> are <u>you</u> from? (addressing "you" formally)
Soy de Venezuela.	<u>I am</u> from Venezuela.
Méjico/México	Mexico
¿De <u>dónde</u> eres <u>tú</u>?	<u>Where</u> are <u>you</u> from? (addressing "you" informally or talking to a child)
Soy de Cuba.	<u>I am</u> from Cuba.
Colombia	Colombia
Honduras	Honduras

You can find a complete list of countries in the Speaking Exercises section at the end of this chapter.

Los números del 1 al 30 *Numbers 1 to 30*

1	uno	11	once	21	veintiuno
2	dos	12	doce	22	veintidós
3	tres	13	trece	23	veintitrés
4	cuatro	14	catorce	24	veinticuatro
5	cinco	15	quince	25	veinticinco
6	seis	16	dieciséis	26	veintiséis
7	siete	17	diecisiete	27	veintisiete
8	ocho	18	dieciocho	28	veintiocho
9	nueve	19	diecinueve	29	veintinueve
10	diez	20	veinte	30	treinta

¿Cuánto tiempo? *How Long?*

Use the numbers above when referring to length of time.

¿Cuánto tiempo hace...?	How long since...? (literally, How much time does it make?)
¿Cuánto tiempo hace que (usted) está aquí?	How long have you been here?
Hace <u>un</u> día.	It has been <u>one</u> day.
mes	month
año	year
<u>una</u> sema<u>na</u>	one week

Observe the plural forms:

dos día<u>s</u>	two day<u>s</u>
tres semana<u>s</u>	three week<u>s</u>
cuatro mes<u>es</u>	four month<u>s</u>
cinco año<u>s</u>	five year<u>s</u>

Preguntando el nombre *Asking Someone His or Her Name*

<u>Cuál es</u> su nombre?	<u>What is</u> your name? (addressing the person formally)
Pedro. Pedro López.	Pedro. Pedro Lopéz.
¿Cuál es <u>su</u> apellido?	What is <u>your</u> last name?
López.	López.

Here's another way of asking someone his or her name formally.

¿Cómo se llama (usted)?	What is your name? (literally, How do you call yourself?)
(Yo) Me llamo Pedro.	My name is Pedro. (literally, I call myself Pedro.)

In an informal situation (such as addressing a young person or child) you can ask:

¿Cómo te llamas (tú)?	What is your name? (How do you call yourself?)
(Yo) Me llamo Pedro.	My name is Pedro. (I call myself Pedro.)

Motivo de la consulta *Reason for Consultation*

¿Cuál es el motivo de su consulta?	What is the reason for your consultation?
¿Cuál es el motivo de su visita?	What is the reason for your visit?
Tengo dolores de cabeza.	I have headaches.
Tengo dolor en el, los, la, las...	I have pain in the...
Tengo dolor de espalda.	I have a backache.
dolor de estómago	a stomachache
dolor en los brazos	pain in the arms
dolor en el pie, en los pies	pain in the foot, in the feet
dolor en la mano, las manos	pain in the hand, the hands
dolor en la cabeza	pain in the head
dolor en la cadera, las caderas	pain in the hip, the hips
dolor en la rodilla, las rodillas	pain in the knee, the knees
dolor en la pierna, las piernas	pain in the leg, the legs
dolor en el cuello	pain in the neck
dolor en el hombro, los hombros	pain in the shoulder, the shoulders

Notice that in Spanish we say "pain in the..." instead of "in my..."

Ocupación y lugar de trabajo *Occupation and Place of Work*

¿Cuál es su ocupación?	What is your job?
Soy médico.	I am a doctor.
¿Dónde trabaja usted?	Where do you work?
Trabajo en un hospital.	I work in a hospital

Let's combine occupation with place of work!

¿Cuál es su ocupación? Soy...	I am...	¿Dónde trabaja usted? Trabajo en...	I work in...
contador, -a	accountant	una oficina	an office
arquitecto, -a	architect	un estudio	a studio
chef	chef	un restaurante	a restaurant
carpintero	handyman, carpenter	construcciones	construction sites
abogado, -a	lawyer	un estudio	a studio
mucama	maid	una casa de familia	a family house
pintor	painter	casas	houses
médico, -a	physician	un hospital	a hospital
profesor, -a	professor	una universidad	a university
recepcionista	receptionist	un hotel	a hotel
secretario, -a	secretary	un consultorio	a doctor's office
cirujano, -a	surgeon	un hospital	a hospital
mesero, -a	waiter, waitress	un restaurante	a restaurant

Exámenes médicos básicos *Basic Medical Tests*

<u>Vamos a hacer</u> **un chequeo general.**	<u>We are going to do</u> a general examination.
un análisis de sangre	a blood test
un análisis de orina	a urine test
un electrocardiograma	an electrocardiogram
una radiografía	an X-ray

Grammar in Use

Second Person Singular Pronoun: *¿usted or tú?*

Usted is the pronoun used to address "you" formally. *Tú* is the pronoun used to address "you" informally. In this book we concentrate on the formal way of addressing people, using **usted** to address the patient, as this is not only the most common but also the most appropriate way to address your patient.

It is highly important to note the verb conjugation for the "formal you," **usted**. **Usted** <u>always</u> takes the verb conjugation of the third person singular *él* (he) and *ella* (she), in all verbs and tenses. See the difference in the previous section between *¿De dónde <u>es</u> usted?* and *¿De dónde <u>eres</u> tú?*

Verb <u>To Be</u>: *ser*

Es (as in "he is") is the third person singular form of the verb *ser* (to be), which is used with the formal "you" pronoun: **usted**. For example: *¿De dónde <u>es</u> usted?*

Eres (as in "you are") is the second person singular of the verb *ser* (to be), which corresponds to the informal "you": *tú*. For example: *¿De dónde <u>eres</u> tú?*

Question Words: *¿Cuál?, ¿Dónde?, ¿Cuánto?*

¿Cuál?   What? Which?

For example:
¿<u>Cuál</u> es su nombre?	<u>What</u> is your name?
¿<u>Cuál</u> es el motivo de la consulta?	<u>What</u> is the reason for your visit?
¿<u>Cuál</u> es su ocupación?	<u>What</u> is your occupation?

¿Dónde?   Where?

For example:
¿De <u>dónde</u> es usted?	<u>Where</u> are you from?

Note also that if you just want to ask "where?" you ask *¿Dónde?* Each time you ask, *¿<u>De</u> dónde es usted?* you are literally asking, "<u>From</u> where are you?"

¿Cuánto?   How much? How long?

For example:
¿<u>Cuánto</u> hace que está aquí?	<u>How long</u> have you been here?

All question words always take an accent in questions and exclamations. Also observe that exclamation and interrogation marks in Spanish are doubled. They open and close the sentence.

> For example:
> **¿Cuál es su nombre?**   What is your name?
> **¡Buenos días!**   Good morning!

Possessive Pronouns: *¿su or tu?*

Observe the questions *¿Cuál es su nombre?* and *¿Cuál es tu nombre?* Both possessive pronouns stand for "your," but *su* corresponds to the formal "you," *usted;* and *tu* corresponds to the informal pronoun *tú.*

Indefinite Articles: *¿un or una?*

Un and *una* correspond to the indefinite article "a." Again, in English we do not have the difficulty of distinguishing articles by gender, but in Spanish this distinction exists. We use *un* with **masculine nouns** and *una* with **feminine nouns.**

Feminine and Masculine Nouns

The gender of some nouns is easily recognized, since the general rule states that nouns ending in *-o* are masculine and those ending in *-a* are feminine. Nevertheless, there are some exceptions, such as *mano* (hand), which is feminine, and *día* (day), which is masculine. Others, such as *agua* (water) and *alma* (soul), which are feminine, are accompanied by the masculine definite article *el* or the masculine indefinite article *un*, since they start with the stressed vowel *a.* Sometimes, distinguishing the gender of certain nouns can give you a hard time, but as a general rule you can consider the following:

- Feminine nouns end in:

    -a: cita (appointment), **cara** (face), **consulta** (consultation)
    -ad: ciudad (city), **igualdad** (equality), **universidad** (university)
    -ción, -sión: emoción (emotion), **pasión** (passion), **atención** (attention)
    -ie: especie (species), **serie** (series), **intemperie** (open-air)
    -ud: salud (health), **quietud** (quietness), **multitud** (crowd)

- Masculine nouns end in:

    -o: codo (elbow), **plato** (plate), **libro** (book)
    -aje: equipaje (luggage), **vendaje** (bandage)
    -or: ardor (ardor, burning), **calor** (heat), **motor** (motor)
    -el: hotel (hotel), **cartel** (sign, chart)

You can refer back to page 3, Chapter 1, to revisit gender regarding health care professions.

Verbs in the Present Tense

hacer   to do, to make

Hace is the third person singular form of the verb *hacer.* Have a look at the word-by-word translation to better understand this sentence structure: *¿Cuánto tiempo <u>hace</u> que (usted) está aquí?* (literally, How much time <u>does it make</u> that you are here?).

The question in Spanish can be then simplified by removing the pronoun *usted,* as in the dialog, just by asking:

¿Cuánto tiempo hace que está aquí?   How long have you been here?

tener   to have

Tengo is the first person singular form of the verb *tener.* It means "I have."

> For example:
> **<u>Tengo</u> dolores de cabeza frecuentes.**   <u>I have</u> frequent headaches.

trabajar   to work

Trabaja is the third person singular form of the verb *trabajar.* It applies to the formal "you," *usted. Trabajo* is the first person singular form of the verb *trabajar.*

> For example:
> **¿Dónde trabaj<u>a</u> usted?**
> **(Yo) Trabaj<u>o</u> en un hospital.**

Remember that since verbs are affected by person and number, you can omit the subject in Spanish, for it is understood or implied.

Future Action

ir   to go

A simple way to show future action is to use the conjugated form of the verb *ir* in the present tense, followed by the preposition *a* (to), followed by any infinitive verb. To express a step to take or something to be done, the doctor can either use the first person ("I," meaning "I, the doctor") or the first person plural ("we," meaning "I, the doctor, and you, the patient"). Observe, then, the first person singular and plural forms of the irregular verb *ir* in the present tense.

voy   <u>I</u> go
vamos   <u>we</u> go

The examples included in this chapter only refer to the plural form *(vamos a...),* while you will see the use of the singular form *(voy a)* in the next chapter.

> For example:
> **<u>Vamos a hacer</u> un chequeo general.**   <u>We are going to do</u> a general examination.
> **<u>Vamos a hacer</u> un análisis de sangre   <u>We are going to do</u> a blood and urine test.
>   y orina.**

You will find more information about verbs in the Verb Reference Section on page 137.

Plural Forms of Nouns

Observe the following nouns in their singular and plural forms:

brazo (arm)   **brazos** (arms)
pierna (leg)   **piernas** (legs)
hombro (shoulder)   **hombros** (shoulders)
cadera (hip)   **caderas** (hips)

As you can see, all these words <u>ending in a vowel sound</u> simply take *-s* to form their plurals. However, there are some rules that can help you with other words that do not end in a vowel sound:

- For <u>words ending in a consonant</u>, we add *-es* to make the plural.

    For example:
    dolor (pain)   **dolores** (pains)
    habitación (room)   **habitaciones** (rooms)
    hospital (hospital)   **hospitales** (hospitals)
    corazón (heart)   **corazones** (hearts)

    Note that the accent in the last syllable of the words ending in *n* or *s* disappears when the new last syllable, in this case indicating plural form, is added.

- For plurals of <u>words ending in z</u>, the *z* is changed into *c*, and *-es* is added.

    For example:
    luz (light)   **luces** (lights)
    pez (fish)   **peces** (fish)

- <u>Words ending in *s*</u> remain unchanged in the plural.

    For example:
    cutis (complexion)   **cutis** (complexions)
    análisis (analysis)   **análisis** (analyses)
    crisis (crisis)   **crisis** (crises)

Definite Articles: *el, la, los, las*

The definite article "the" takes four different forms in Spanish: *el, la, los,* and *las.*

- **el:** masculine singular

    For example: **el brazo** (the arm), **el enfermero** (the male nurse), **el hombro** (the shoulder)

- **la:** feminine singular

    For example: **la pierna** (the leg), **la cadera** (the hip), **la secretaria** (the secretary)

- **los:** masculine plural

    For example: **los brazos** (the arms), **los hombros** (the shoulders), **los pies** (the feet)

- **las:** feminine plural

    For example: **las semanas** (the weeks), **las caderas** (the hips), **las piernas** (the legs)

Speaking Exercises

1. Listen to the dialog **"Primera visita al médico"** again (CD track 6). Then go to page 7 and practice reading the dialog, changing the information provided by the patient each time you read.

2. In the following example, María López is introducing herself. Listen to her, then read aloud.

    Mi nombre es María López. Soy enfermera. Soy de Puerto Rico. Trabajo en un hospital.

    Can you do the same to introduce yourself? To do this without the CD, use the following prompts:

    Nombre:

    _____

    Profesión, ocupación:

    _____

    País de origen:

    _____

    Lugar de trabajo:

    _____

    Can you provide all this information in four sentences as María López did before? Suppose you are at a medical convention and it is your turn to introduce yourself. Give your name and your profession or occupation, and say where you are from and where you work.
    Ready? Look at Maria's example for help.

3. Dialog: In the following dialog, the doctor is asking the patient some questions on his first office visit. Give the patient's replies. Try to provide complete answers.

    D: **¿Cuál es su nombre?**
    P: (Say your name is Ramón Báez.)
    D: **¿De dónde es usted?**
    P: (Say you are from Ecuador.)
    D: **¿Cuánto tiempo hace que está aquí?**
    P: (Say you have been here for two years.)
    D: **¿Cuál es el motivo de su visita?**
    P: (Say you have backaches and pain in your shoulders.)
    D: **¿Cuál es su ocupación?**
    P: (Say you are a waiter.)
    D: **¿Dónde trabaja usted?**
    P: (Say you work in a restaurant.)

4. Practice nationalities by reading aloud! Observe the *-o, -a* endings. Adjectives of nationality end in *-o* when referring to a male and in *-a* when referring to a female.

¿De dónde es usted?	¿Cuál es su nacionalidad?
Soy de Argentina	**Soy argentino, -a**
Brasil	**brasileño, -a**
Chile	**chileno, -a**
Colombia	**colombiano, -a**
Costa Rica	**costarricense**
Cuba	**cubano, -a**
El Salvador	**salvadoreño, -a**
Guatemala	**guatemalteco, -a**
Honduras	**hondureño, -a**
Méjico, México	**mejicano, -a; mexicano, -a**
Panamá	**panameño, -a**
Perú	**peruano, -a**
Puerto Rico	**puertorriqueño, -a; portorriqueño, -a**
República Dominicana	**dominicano, -a**
Venezuela	**venezolano, -a**

Written Exercises

1. Write a paragraph about yourself using your personal information from Speaking Exercise 2.

_____

_____

_____

_____

2. Complete the questions with *cuál* or *dónde* and match them with their corresponding answers.

¿(a)_____ es su nombre?   (1) Trabajo en un supermercado.

¿(b)_____ trabaja usted?   (2) Tengo dolor de estómago.

¿De (c)_____ es usted?   (3) Mi nombre es Juan Díaz.

¿(d)_____ es su profesión?   (4) Soy asociado médico.

¿(e)_____ es el motivo de su visita? (5) Soy panameño.

3. Complete the doctor's part in the following dialog.

      D: Buenos días. ¿(a)_____ es el motivo de su visita?

      P: Tengo dolores musculares.

      D: ¿(b)_____ tiene los dolores?

      P: En la espalda y en las piernas.

      D: ¿(c) _____ trabaja usted?

      P: Trabajo en un restaurante. Soy mesera.

      D: ¿De (d) _____ es usted?

      P: Soy de Panamá.

      D: ¡Oh! ¿(e)_____ que está aquí?

      P: Hace dos años.

      D: Bien, veamos...

4. Complete the following chart with the feminine form of the adjectives to indicate nationality. Remember to change the *o* for *a,* and add *a* and take off the accent when the word ends in *s* or *n.* Adjectives ending in *e* remain unchanged. Note that nationalities in Spanish do not take capital letters. When in doubt while you are speaking with someone, you can still choose to use the country of origin, for example: ***María es de Ecuador,*** instead of ***María es ecuatoriana.***

País *Country*	**Nacionalidad** *Nationality* (male)	(female)
Argentina	argentino	_____
Alemania	alemán	_____
Brasil	brasileño	_____
Chile	chileno	_____
Colombia	colombiano	_____
Cuba	cubano	_____
El Salvador	salvadoreño	_____
Estados Unidos de América	estadounidense	_____
	(americano)	_____
Francia	francés	_____

Grecia	griego	_____
Honduras	hondureño	_____
Inglaterra	inglés	_____
Nicaragua	nicaragüense	_____
Perú	peruano	_____
Puerto Rico	puertorriqueño	_____
Venezuela	venezolano	_____

5. Now complete the following sentences with names of famous people or people you know with that nationality. Then write two similar sentences.

> For example:
> **María es colombiana.**
> **Fernando es argentino.**

_____ es puertorriqueño.

_____ es brasileño.

_____ es americana.

_____

_____

6. Translate the time expressions.

two months	(a)_____
thirty-nine weeks	(b)_____
ten years	(c)_____
seis meses	(d)_____
quince días	(e)_____
tres años	(f)_____

 **Role-Playing Exercise**

Entrevistando a un nuevo paciente *Interviewing a New Patient*

In the following situation you are a physician working in your consulting office. A new patient has come to see you. You have to establish a first contact with the patient and find out what is wrong with him. Play the CD track (10) and interact with the patient. You can also practice this activity without the CD, following the prompts below.

You: (Ask his name.)
P: **Mi nombre es Juan Pereyra.**
You: (Ask about his country of origin.)
P: **Soy de Honduras.**
You: (Ask how long he has been here.)
P: **¡Oh, doctor! Hace veintitrés años que estoy aquí en los Estados Unidos.**
You: (Ask the reason for his office visit.)
P: **¡Ay doctor! Es que tengo muchos dolores musculares y dolores de cabeza. Tengo muchos dolores aquí en los brazos y en la espalda.**
You: (Ask about his occupation and place of work.)
P: **Soy empleado. Trabajo en un banco.**
You: (Tell him that you are going to do a general examination.)

You can continue creating new situations by incorporating new and more specific vocabulary from the Medical Specialties section in Appendix 1 (page 129).

Cultural Information

Many Latin patients will feel more confident if they can exchange some kind of conversation with their physicians, especially if this is their first office visit. Many Latin patients are talkative, and they will sometimes accompany their narration with extra or small details in an attempt to provide complete and descriptive information.

Chapter 3

En la sala de emergencias

In the Emergency Room

In this chapter, you will learn how to ask your patient his or her address, telephone number, medical insurance, and social security number. You will also learn how to deal with a chief complaint in an emergency room situation, prescribe and indicate medicines, and inform the patient of required tests or exams. In addition, you will continue practicing all you have learned in the previous chapter and find out about cultural issues that may arise in an emergency room setting.

Dialog: El Sr. Benito Gómez tiene dolor en el pecho

Mr. Benito Gómez Has Chest Pain

 La recepcionista del hospital atiende al Sr. Benito Gómez.
The hospital receptionist takes care of Mr. Benito Gómez.

Recepcionista:	**¿Cuál es su nombre?**
Paciente:	**Benito Gómez.**
Recepcionista:	**Disculpe, ¿cuál es su apellido?**
Paciente:	**Gómez.**
Recepcionista:	**¿Cuál es su domicilio?**
Paciente:	**7100 SW 126 Street.***
Recepcionista:	**¿Cuál es su teléfono?**
Paciente:	**(304) 456-09876.**
Recepcionista:	**¿Cuál es su seguro médico?**
Paciente:	**"Salud de la Familia."**
Recepcionista:	**¿Su número de seguro social, por favor?**
Paciente:	**123-456-987-65X.**
Recepcionista:	**¿Cuál es el motivo de su consulta?**
Paciente:	**Tengo mucho dolor en el pecho y palpitaciones.**
Recepcionista:	**¿Tiene alergias? ¿Es alérgico a alguna medicina?**
Paciente:	**No.**
Recepcionista:	**Bien. Espere aquí.**

---

* Generally, Spanish-speaking patients give address references such as "Street," "SW," etc., in English. The term that they are more likely to translate in Spanish is "street," *calle.* For example, the patient might also say, *Mi domicilio es 7100 SW 126 calle.*

Con el médico de emergencias *With the Emergency Room Doctor*

Doctor: **¿Cuáles son sus síntomas?**
Paciente: **Doctor, tengo mucho dolor en el pecho y palpitaciones.**
Doctor: **¿Dónde tiene el dolor exactamente?**
Paciente: **Aquí, doctor.**
Doctor: **¿Cuánto hace que tiene este dolor en el pecho?**
Paciente: **Hace aproximadamente dos horas, pero ahora es más intenso.**
Doctor: **Veamos... bien, vamos a hacer un electrocardiograma. Recuéstese en la camilla, por favor.**

Dialog Comprehension

Test your comprehension of the dialog by checking the correct options below.

Benito Gómez es el nombre del:
   paciente   ☐
   médico   ☐
   seguro médico   ☐

Seguro social means:
   social security   ☐
   telephone number   ☐
   medical insurance   ☐

"Salud de la Familia" es su:
   teléfono   ☐
   seguro médico   ☐
   seguro social   ☐

7100 SW 126 Street es su:
   teléfono   ☐
   domicilio, dirección   ☐
   nombre   ☐

Vocabulary Practice

In this section you will find words and phrases necessary to take care of your patients in an emergency room scenario.

Datos personales del paciente *Patient's Personal Information*

¿Cuál es su nombre?	What is your name?
apellido?	last name?
domicilio, dirección?	address?
código postal?	zip code?
número de teléfono?	telephone number?
seguro médico?	medical insurance?
número de seguro social?	social security number?
fecha de nacimiento?	birth date?

For example:

Mi nombre es Benito Gómez.	<u>My</u> name <u>is</u> Benito Gómez.
Mi apellido es Gómez.	My last name is Gómez.
Mi domicilio es 7100 SW 126 Street.	My address is 7100 SW 126th Street.
Mi (número de) teléfono es (304) 456-09876.	My telephone number is (304) 456-09876.
Mi seguro médico es "Salud de la Familia".	My medical insurance is "Salud de la Familia."
Mi número de seguro social es 123-456-987-65X.	My social security number is 123-456-987-65X.
Mi fecha de nacimiento es 20 de marzo de 1961.	My birth date is March 20, 1961.

Acerca de dolores y síntomas *Regarding Pains and Symptoms*

¿Cuáles son sus síntomas?	What are your symptoms?
¿Qué siente?	What do you feel?
¿Qué le pasa?	What is happening (to you)? (literally, "What happens to you?")
Tengo dolor en el pecho.	I have a pain in my chest.
dolor abdominal	abdominal pain
sangre en el excremento	blood in the stool
dificultad para respirar	breathing difficulty
dolor en el pecho	chest pain
un resfrío, un resfriado	a cold
estreñimiento	constipation
tos	a cough
calambres	cramps
diarrea	diarrhea
malestares	discomforts
mareos	dizziness
dolor de oído	an earache

fiebre	fever
gripe, gripa	flu
dolor de cabeza	headache
indigestión	indigestion
náuseas	nausea
palpitaciones	palpitations
una erupción	a rash
falta de aire	shortness of breath
dolor de garganta	sore throat
dolor de estómago	stomachache
temperatura	temperature
opresión en el pecho	tightness in the chest
vómitos	vomiting
vómitos con sangre	blood in the vomit
tos con flema	wet cough, cough with phlegm

Accidentes *Accidents*

¿Qué le ocurrió?, ¿Qué le pasó?	What happened to you?
Me quemé.	I burned myself.
Me quemé el brazo.	I burned my arm.
el dedo	finger
la mano	hand
la muñeca	wrist
Me corté.	I cut myself.
Choqué.	I crashed.
Choqué con un carro.	I crashed into a car.
un árbol	a tree
una pared	a wall
Me golpeé.	I bumped into something; I hit myself.
Me golpeé con una puerta.	I bumped into a door.
un árbol	a tree
una pared	a wall
una ventana	a window
Me caí.	I fell.
Me caí de las escaleras.	I fell down the stairs.
Me caí en la calle.	I fell in the street.
Me fracturé (un hueso).	I fractured (a bone).
Me lastimé.	I hurt myself.
Tuve un accidente de carro.	I had a car accident.
Me mordió un animal.	An animal bit me.
un perro	A dog
un gato	A cat
una serpiente	A snake
un murciélago	A bat
un mapache	A racoon
Me picó un insecto.	An insect stung, bit me.
una abeja	A bee
un mosquito	A mosquito
una araña	A spider
una avispa	A wasp

Indicando análisis, exámenes, pruebas *Indicating Analyses, Exams, Tests*

Vamos a hacer un chequeo general.	We are going to do a general examination.
un análisis de sangre	a blood test
una colonoscopía	a colonoscopy
una tomografía computada	a CT scan
un electrocardiograma	an electrocardiogram
un electroencefalograma	an electroencephalogram
un enema	an enema
una resonancia magnética	an MRI
una prueba de esputo	a sputum test
un cultivo de garganta	a throat culture
una ecografía, un ultrasonido	an ultrasound
un análisis de orina	a urine test
una radiografía	an X-ray

Indicando medicinas, medicamentos *Indicating Medicines*

<u>**Voy a darle...**</u>	<u>I am going to</u> give you...
Voy a prescribirle...	I am going to prescribe you...
acetaminofeno	acetaminophen
un analgésico	an analgesic
un antiácido	an antacid
un antialérgico	an antiallergic drug
un antibiótico	an antibiotic
un antihistamínico	an antihistamine
aspirina	aspirin
codeína	codeine
cortisona	cortisone
ibuprofeno	ibuprofen
insulina	insulin
morfina	morphine
penicilina	penicillin
vitaminas	vitamins

Presentación de la medicina *Medicine Presentation*

cápsulas	capsules
crema	cream
gotas	drops
inyecciones	injections
loción	lotion
pastillas	lozenges/tablets
ungüento	ointment
comprimidos	pills
píldoras	pills
spray	spray
supositorio	suppository
jarabe	syrup
tabletas	tablets

Más vocabulario en la sala de emergencias *More Emergency Room Vocabulary*

Start just by getting familiar with these words. You will see how you will gradually incorporate them to your dialogs!

banda adhesiva	adhesive bandage
cinta adhesiva	adhesive tape
alcohol	alcohol
alergia	allergy
ambulancia	ambulance
mordedura de animal	animal bite
apendicitis	appendicitis
vendaje	bandage
transfusión de sangre	blood transfusion
huesos	bones
yeso	cast
muletas	crutches
guantes descartables	disposable gloves
fractura	fracture
gasa	gauze
anestesia general	general anesthesia
hemorragia	hemorrhage
agua oxigenada	hydrogen peroxide
lesión	injury
terapia intensiva	intensive care
intoxicación	intoxication
hidratación intravenosa	intravenous hydration
anestesia local	local anesthesia
operación	operation
sobredosis	overdose
oxígeno	oxygen
rabia	rabies
otoscopio	otoscope
solución salina	saline solution
suero	serum
estetoscopio	stethoscope
puntos	stitches
camilla	stretcher, examining table
camillero	stretcher bearer
cirugía	surgery
hisopo	swab
tétano, antitetánica	tetanus, tetanus booster
vacuna	vaccine
signos vitales	vital signs
silla de ruedas	wheelchair

Instrucciones útiles *Useful Commands*

Respire; No respire.	Breathe; Don't breathe.
Respire profundo.	Breathe deeply (take a deep breath).
Haga estos ejercicios para su...	Do these exercises for your...
No haga tareas pesadas.	Don't do heavy tasks.
Levántese.	Get up.
Mantenga el aire.	Hold your breath.
Haga vida normal.	Lead a normal life.
Recuéstese en la camilla.	Lie down on the stretcher.
No levante peso.	Don't lift heavy objects.
Haga una cita con...	Make an appointment with...
Mueva...; No mueva...	Move...; Don't move...
No se mueva.	Don't move (yourself).
Abra la boca.	Open your mouth.
Levante el brazo derecho.	Raise your right arm.
el brazo izquierdo	your left arm
la pierna derecha	your right leg
la pierna izquierda	your left leg
Siéntese.	Sit down.
Haga reposo.	Rest; Stay at rest.
Tome esta medicina.	Take this medicine.
Saque la lengua.	Stick out your tongue.
Espere aquí; Aguarde aquí.	Wait here.
No se preocupe.	Don't worry.

It's helpful to practice some of the new vocabulary by relating the word to the real object! When at home, go to your medicine cabinet and practice by saying the Spanish words for the objects you see. It will be even better if you actually touch or grasp the object while you do this exercise. You can enlarge this experience by going to a pharmacy, standing in a medicine aisle at a supermarket, or even looking for different objects at your workplace, if you find some time. If you come across an object that is not in this chapter, go to a dictionary for help. This is also a great way to enlarge your vocabulary!

Grammar in Use

Agreement in Number

In Spanish, it is important that the question word, noun, possessive pronoun, and verb agree in number.

For example:	
¿Cuál es su nombre?	What is your <u>name</u>?
¿Cuáles son sus síntomas?	What are your <u>symptoms</u>?

Possessive Adjective

mi   my

For example:	
Mi nombre es Benito Gómez.	My name is Benito Gómez.
Mi dirección es 7100 SW 126 Street.	My address is 7100 SW 126 Street.

Verbs

As you review the examples in this section, remember that pronouns can be omitted in Spanish, as the verb conjugations themselves indicate the person.

VERBS IN THE PRESENT TENSE

pasar   to happen
pasa (third person singular)   it happens

> For example:
> **¿Qué le pasa?**   What is happening (to you)? (literally, "<u>What happens</u> to you?")

sentir   to feel
siente (third person singular)   you (formal) feel; he, she feels
siento (first person singular)   I feel

> For example:
> **¿Qué <u>siente</u>?**   What <u>do you feel</u>?
> **<u>Siento</u> un dolor muy fuerte aquí.**   <u>I feel</u> a very strong pain here.

tener   to have
tiene (third person singular)   you (formal) have; he, she has
tengo (first person singular)   I have

> For example:
> **¿Dónde <u>tiene</u> el dolor exactamente?**   Where exactly do <u>you have</u> the pain?
> **<u>Tengo</u> dolor en el pecho.**   <u>I have</u> a pain in my chest.

VERBS IN THE PAST TENSE

ocurrir   to occur, to happen
ocurri<u>ó</u> (third person singular)   occurred, happened

> For example:
> **¿Qué le <u>ocurrió</u>?**   <u>What</u> <u>happened</u> to you?

Here, the object pronoun *le* is used to show the action that happened "to you."

chocar   to crash
choqu<u>é</u> (first person singular)   I crashed

tener   to have
tuv<u>e</u> (first person singular)   I had
tuv<u>o</u> (third person singular)   you (formal), he, she had

> For example:
> **<u>Tuve</u> un accidente de carro.**   <u>I had</u> a car accident.
> **El Sr. Pérez <u>tuvo</u> una reacción alérgica.**   Mr. Pérez <u>had</u> an allergic reaction.

morder   to bite
mordi<u>ó</u> (third person singular)   you (formal), he, she, it bit

> For example:
> **<u>Me mordió</u> un animal.**   An animal <u>bit me</u>.
> **<u>Me mordió</u> un perro.**   A dog <u>bit me</u>.

picar	to bite (for insects), to sting
pic<u>ó</u> (third person singular)	you (formal), he, she, it bit/stung

For example:

<u>Me pic</u><u>ó</u> un mosquito.	A mosquito <u>bit me</u>.
<u>Me pic</u><u>ó</u> una abeja.	A bee <u>stung me</u>.

It will be meaningful to mention, just to avoid confusions with the reflexive pronoun *me* introduced right afterwards, that in these last two examples, *me* functions as an object pronoun. As you can see, in these examples the object pronoun *me* corresponds to "me" as the object of the verb.

REFLEXIVE VERBS IN THE PAST TENSE

The verbs in this chapter used to describe accidents are used with the <u>reflexive pronoun for first person singular</u> *me* to show that the receiver of the action is the person talking, "myself." However, if we want to use these verbs to ask the patient questions, or to describe what happened to the patient, or to someone else, we need to use the <u>reflexive pronoun for the third person singular</u> *se*, "yourself (formal you)," "himself," "herself." Reflexive verbs take the reflexive pronoun *se* <u>after the verb</u> in their infinitive forms. However, reflexive pronouns are placed <u>before the verb</u> when conjugated.

quemar(se)	to burn (oneself)
quemé (first person singular)	I burned
quem<u>ó</u> (third person singular)	you (formal), he, she burned...

For example:

<u>Me</u> quemé.	I burned myself.
<u>Me</u> quemé el brazo con la sartén.	I burned my arm with the frying pan.
El paciente Martínez <u>se</u> quem<u>ó</u> el dedo.	Patient Martínez burned his finger.

cortar(se)	to cut (oneself)
cort<u>é</u> (first person singular)	I cut
cort<u>ó</u> (third person singular)	you (formal), he, she cut...

For example:

<u>Me</u> cort<u>é</u> el dedo con un cuchillo.	I cut my finger with a knife.
El Sr. Pérez <u>se</u> cort<u>ó</u> el dedo con un abridor de latas.	Mr. Pérez cut his finger with a can opener.

golpear(se)	to hit (oneself)
golpe<u>é</u> (first person singular)	I hit, I bumped
golpe<u>ó</u> (third person singular)	you (formal), he, she hit, bumped...

For example:

<u>Me</u> golpe<u>é</u> contra una pared.	I hit myself against a wall.
El paciente López <u>se</u> golpe<u>ó</u> la cabeza.	Patient López bumped his head.

fracturar(se)	to fracture (oneself)
fractur<u>é</u> (first person singular)	I fractured...
fractur<u>ó</u> (third person singular)	you (formal), he, she fractured...

For example:

¿<u>Me</u> fractur<u>é</u> algo, doctor?	Did I fracture anything, doctor?
El paciente Vélez <u>se</u> fractur<u>ó</u> la pierna.	Patient Vélez fractured his leg.

lastimar(se)	to hurt (oneself)
lastimé (first person singular)	I hurt…
lastimó (third person singular)	you (formal), he, she hurt…

For example:

Me lastimé el brazo.	I hurt my arm.
¿Cuándo se lastimó?	When did you hurt yourself?
El paciente José Díaz se lastimó el codo.	Patient José Díaz hurt his elbow.

caer(se)	to fall (oneself)
caí (first person singular)	I fell down
cayó (third person singular)	you (formal), he, she fell down

For example:

Me caí de las escaleras.	I fell down the stairs.
El paciente Fuentes se cayó de la silla.	Patient Fuentes fell off the chair.

You will find more information about verbs in the past tense in the Verb Reference Section on page 137. You will also find more references to Reflexive Verbs in Chapters 9 and 10.

FUTURE ACTION

ir	to go
vamos (first person plural)	We go
vamos a + infinitive	We are going to + infinitive

(Refer back to Chapter 2, page 13, to review this information.)

For example:

Vamos a hacer un electrocardiograma.	We are going to do an EKG.
Vamos a hacer una radiografía.	We are going to take an X-ray.

voy (first person singular)	I go
voy a + infinitive	I am going to + infinitive

For example:

Voy a prescribirle una medicina.	I am going to prescribe you a medicine.
Voy a darle un antitérmico.	I am going to give you an antitermic.

The *le* particle is the indirect object pronoun *le* that corresponds to the indirect object of the action. It means "to, for you."

Compare:

Voy a prescribirle un antibiótico.	I am going to prescribe <u>you</u> an antibiotic.
Vamos a ponerle un yeso.	We are going to put a cast on <u>you</u>.
Voy a prescribirle un antihistamínico.	I am going to prescribe <u>you</u> an antihistamine.

COMMAND FORMS

It is important to learn how to give instructions to your patients. Let's consider the verbs used in their infinitive forms and observe how you change them to give your patients common commands in the emergency room.

respirar	to breathe

For example:

Respire profundo.	Breathe (deeply); Take a deep breath.
No respire.	Don't breathe.

hacer   to do, to make

> For example:
> **No haga tareas pesadas.**   Don't do heavy tasks.
> **Haga vida normal.**   Lead a normal life.
> **Haga una cita con el especialista.**   Make an appointment with the specialist.

levantarse   to get up

> For example:
> **Levántese.**   Get up.

mantener   to hold, to keep

> For example:
> **Mantenga el aire.**   Hold your breath.

recostarse   to lie down

> For example:
> **Recuéstese en la camilla.**   Lie down on the stretcher.

mover(se)   to move

> For example:
> **No se mueva.**   Don't move (yourself).
> **Mueva la cabeza.**   Move your head.
> **No mueva la espalda.**   Don't move your back.

abrir   to open

> For example:
> **Abra la boca.**   Open your mouth.

levantar   to put up, raise

> For example:
> **Levante el brazo derecho.**   Put up, raise your right arm.
> **   la pierna izquierda**   your left leg

sentarse   to sit

> For example:
> **Siéntese.**   Sit down.

tomar   to take

> For example:
> **Tome esta medicina.**   Take this medicine.

sacar   to take out, stick out

> For example:
> **Saque la lengua.**   Stick out your tongue.

esperar   to wait

> For example:
> **Espere aquí.**   Wait here.

preocuparse   to worry

> For example:
> **No se preocupe.**   Don't worry.

Speaking Exercises

1. Listen to the dialog **"El Sr. Benito Gómez tiene dolor en el pecho"** again (CD track 11). You will notice how much more familiar it will sound to you now! Then go to page 20 and practice reading the dialog, changing the patient's information.

2. Mr. Pereyra is at a hospital admission desk. Play the role of the receptionist asking for his personal information and complete the following form with his personal data (CD track 14).

Apellido del paciente: _____

Nombre: _____

Domicilio: _____

Teléfono: _____

Seguro social: _____

Seguro médico: _____

3. Practice different emergency room situations. You can pick items from the vocabulary lists below for help.

DIALOG PROMPTS:

D: **¿Cuáles son sus síntomas?¿Qué le pasó?¿Qué le ocurrió?**
P: **Tengo...** (symptoms) **Me..., Tuve..., Choqué...** (accidents)
D: **Vamos a hacer un, una...** (test or exam)
P: **Bien, doctor.**
D: **Voy a prescribirle...** (medicine)

VOCABULARY FOR SYMPTOMS:

calambres	diarrea	dificultad para respirar
dolor de cabeza	dolor de espalda	dolor de estómago
dolor de garganta	dolor de oído	dolor de pecho
dolor en el apéndice	una erupción	falta de aire
fiebre	indigestión	malestares
mareos	náuseas	opresión en el pecho
palpitaciones	sangre en el excremento	temperatura
tos	vómitos	vómitos con sangre

VOCABULARY FOR ACCIDENTS:

Choqué...	Me caí...	Me mordió un...
Me corté...	Me fracturé	Me picó un insecto.
Me golpeé...	Me lastimé	Tuve un accidente.
Me quemé...	Choqué con...	Me lastimé con...

VOCABULARY FOR ANALYSES, TESTS, AND EXAMS:

análisis de sangre	colonoscopía	ultrasonido (diagnóstico)
ecografía	electrocardiograma	tomografía computada
electroencefalograma	enema	prueba de esputo
hisopado de garganta	radiografía	resonancia magnética

VOCABULARY FOR MEDICINES:

acetaminofeno	análgesico	antiácido
antialérgico	antibiótico	antihistamínico
aspirina	codeína	cortisona
ibuprofeno	insulina	morfina
penicilina	antitetánica	vitaminas

Written Exercises

1. Write the corresponding number in the blank.

    Nombre   (a)_____   1. (305)197-23324

    Domicilio   (b)_____   2. 04042-345-986XX

    Teléfono   (c)_____   3. Marisela

    Seguro médico   (d)_____   4. 63032 NW 123 calle

    Seguro social   (e)_____   5. dolor de estómago, fiebre y vómitos

    Motivo de la consulta   (f)_____   6. Health Salud

2. Now, complete the dialog between the receptionist and patient Díaz.

    R: ¿Cuál es su (a)_____?

    P: Marisela Díaz.

    R: ¿(b)_____ es su domicilio?

    P: 63032 NW 123 calle

    R: ¿Cuál (c)_____ su seguro médico?

    P: Health Salud.

    R: ¿Cuál es su (d)_____?

    P: 04042-345-986XX

    R: ¿(e)_____?

    P: Tengo dolor de estómago, fiebre y vómitos.

3. Patient Amelia Vargas goes to an emergency room after she fell in the street. Complete the following dialog between patient Vargas and the receptionist. Pick from the words below; they can be used more than once.

¿Cuál es...?	¿Cuánto hace...?	soy	caí	domicilio
motivo	tengo	es	qué	hacer

R: Buenos días. ¿(a)_____ su apellido, por favor?

P: Vargas.

R: ¿Su nombre?

P: Amelia.

R: Muy bien. ¿(b)_____ le pasó?

P: Me (c)_____ en la calle.

R: Bien. Necesito algunos datos. ¿Cuál es su (d)_____?

P: 2932 NW 31st Street.

R: Y, ¿(e)_____ su número de teléfono?

P: (304) 123-987650.

R: ¿(f)_____ su ocupación?

P: (g)_____ empleada en un supermercado.

R: ¿(h)_____ usted alérgica a alguna medicina?

P: No.

R: Espere aquí. Ya la atiende el médico de guardia.

Con el médico de guardia

D: Bien, ¿Dónde se cayó?

P: Me (i)_____ en la calle. Doctor, tengo mucho dolor en la rodilla.

D: A ver..., bien, vamos a (j)_____ una radiografía.

P: Bien, doctor.

Role-Playing Exercise

En la sala de emergencias *In the Emergency Room*

In the following situation, Mr. González has a sudden pain and tightness in his chest. He also has difficulty breathing, so he goes to the emergency room where <u>you work as a health care professional</u>. The receptionist collects his personal information data, then you interview your patient. Play the CD track (15) and listen to the dialog between the patient and the receptionist, then interact with your patient.

You:	(Greet your patient, Mr. González. It's 11 P.M.)
P:	**Buenas noches.**
You:	(Ask the patient what happened to him.)
P:	**Tengo un dolor muy fuerte en el pecho, también siento como una opresión y dificultad para respirar.**
You:	(Ask him if he is allergic to any medicine.)
P:	**No, no soy alérgico a ninguna medicina.**
You:	(Ask how long he has had the pain.)
P:	**Hace dos horas aproximadamente.**
You:	(Tell him you are going to do an EKG.)
P:	**Bien.**

Cultural Information

In an emergency room situation, a Spanish-speaking patient may have certain distinctive characteristics due to the simple fact of a difference in culture. This is sometimes translated into extra anxiety, impatience, or uncertainty, and occasional loud conversations with family members. The support provided by the environment and the personal attitudes of the health care providers, such as eye contact, explanatory comments, and attitudes showing care and concern, play an essential role to help both patient and family handle the situation in a more positive way.

Chapter 4

Presentando a colegas

Introducing Colleagues

In this chapter you will learn how to introduce other people and colleagues, and to provide information about them such as their name, nationality, profession, medical specialty, marital status, country or city of residence, place of work, and languages spoken.

Dialog: En una convención médica

At a Medical Convention

 El Dr. Martín Ramírez está conociendo a sus colegas, con quienes comparte un proyecto. La Dra. Iris Fuentes, coordinadora en esta convención, los presenta.
Dr. Martín Ramírez is getting to know his colleagues, with whom he shares a project. Dr. Iris Fuentes, the convention coordinator, introduces them to one another.

Iris Fuentes:	**El Dr. Juan Luppi es médico obstetra. Él trabaja en el Hospital General, en Chile. Habla español e inglés y vive en Santiago de Chile.**
Todos:	**Mucho gusto.**
Juan Luppi:	**¡Encantado!**
Iris Fuentes:	**Marta Vallesteros es asociado médico. Ella también trabaja en el Hospital General en Chile. Marta habla español e inglés y también vive en Santiago de Chile.**
Todos:	**Hola, un placer.**
Iris Fuentes:	**La Dra. Carmen Gutiérrez es cardióloga. Trabaja en el hospital Mayor de Barcelona, España. Ella habla español, inglés y francés.**
Todos:	**Mucho gusto.**
C. Gutiérrez:	**Un placer.**
Iris Fuentes:	**La Dra. Akiko Sato es dermatóloga. Ella es japonesa y trabaja en una clínica en Tokio. Akiko habla japonés y español.**
Todos:	**Encantado/Encantada.**
Akiko Sato:	**Un gusto.**

Iris Fuentes:	**El Dr. Michel Spencer es gastroenterólogo. Él es francés y trabaja en el Hospital Central de París.**
Todos:	**Mucho gusto.**
M. Spencer:	**Un placer.**
Iris Fuentes:	**Bien. Vamos a presentar los objetivos del proyecto.**

Dialog Comprehension

Test your comprehension of the dialog by checking the correct options.

¿Dónde trabaja el Dr. Juan Luppi?

en el Hospital General en Chile ☐

en el Hospital Mayor en España ☐

en una clínica en Japón ☐

La Dra. Akiko Sato es:

cardióloga ☐

dermatóloga ☐

gastroenteróloga ☐

Marta Vallesteros es:

enfermera ☐

dermatóloga ☐

asociado médico ☐

El Dr. Michel Spencer es:

hematólogo ☐

infectólogo ☐

gastroenterólogo ☐

Vocabulary Practice

In this section you will find words and phrases necessary to introduce other people.

Presentando a un hombre *Introducing a Man*

Él es...	He is...
Él es el Dr. Juan Luppi.	He is Dr. Juan Luppi.
Él es el Dr. Michel Spencer.	He is Dr. Michel Spencer.

Presentando a una mujer *Introducing a Woman*

<u>Ella</u> es...	<u>She</u> is...
<u>Ella</u> es la asociado médico Marta Vallesteros.	<u>She</u> is P.A. Marta Vallesteros.
<u>Ella</u> es la Dra. Carmen Gutiérrez.	<u>She</u> is Dr. Carmen Gutiérrez.
<u>Ella</u> es la Dra. Akiko Sato.	<u>She</u> is Dr. Akiko Sato.

Especialidades médicas *Medical Specialties*

alergista	allergist
anestesiólogo, -a	anesthesiologist
cardiólogo, -a	cardiologist
quiropráctico, -a	chiropractor
dermatólogo, -a	dermatologist
endocrinólogo, -a	endocrinologist
gastroenterólogo, -a	gastroenterologist
médico general	general physician
gerontólogo, -a	gerontologist
ginecólogo, -a	gynecologist
hematólogo, -a	hematologist
nefrólogo, -a	nephrologist
neurólogo, -a	neurologist
obstetra	obstetrician
oncólogo, -a	oncologist
ortopedista, especialista en ortopedia	orthopedist
otolaringólogo, -a	otolaryngologist
pediatra	pediatrician
podiatra, especialista en podiatría	podiatrist
psiquiatra	psychiatrist
psicólogo, -a	psychologist
especialista en afecciones respiratorias	respiratory-care physician
cirujano, -a	surgeon
urólogo, -a	urologist

Presentando a una especialista mujer *Introducing a Female Specialist*

<u>Ella</u> es...	<u>She</u> is...
<u>Ella</u> es cardiólo<u>ga</u>.	<u>She</u> is a cardiologist.
cirujan<u>a</u>	surgeon
dermatólo<u>ga</u>	dermatologist
psicólo<u>ga</u>	psychologist
obste<u>tra</u>	obstetrician

Presentando a un especialista hombre *Introducing a Male Specialist*

Él es...   He is...
Él es cirujano.   He is a surgeon.
    neurólogo   neurologist
    urólogo   urologist
    psiquiatra   psychiatrist

Lugares de trabajo *Places of Work*

Él, Ella trabaja en...   He, She works in...
    una clínica   a clinic
    una clínica de cirugía cosmética   a cosmetic surgery clinic
    un centro quiropráctico   a chiropractic center
    un centro de dermatología   a dermatology center
    un centro de educación especial   a special education center
    un centro de salud   a health care center
    un hospital   a hospital
    un laboratorio   a laboratory
    un hogar de ancianos   a nursing home
    un consultorio médico privado   a private medical office
    un centro de rehabilitación   a rehabilitation center
    un instituto de investigación   a research institute

Idiomas *Languages*

Él, Ella habla...   He, She speaks...
    chino   Chinese
    inglés   English
    francés   French
    alemán   German
    italiano   Italian
    japonés   Japanese
    coreano   Korean
    portugués   Portuguese
    español   Spanish
    vietnamés   Vietnamese

Please refer to a dictionary for more vocabulary related to languages.

Países y ciudades capitales *Countries and Capital Cities*

Él, Ella vive en...   He, She lives in...
    Argentina/Buenos Aires   Argentina/Buenos Aires
    Canadá/Ottawa   Canada/Ottawa
    China/Beijing   China/Beijing
    Colombia/Bogotá   Colombia/Bogota
    Cuba/La Habana   Cuba/Havana
    Inglaterra/Londres   England/London

Francia/París	France/Paris
Méjico, México/Méjico, México	Mexico/Mexico City
Puerto Rico/San Juan	Puerto Rico/San Juan
España/Madrid	Spain/Madrid
Estados Unidos/Washington, D.C.	United States/Washington, D.C.

Please refer to Chapter 2 or a dictionary or atlas for more country names and capital cities.

Estado civil *Marital Status*

Él es...	He is...
Ella es...	She is...
soltero, -a	single
casado, -a	married
separado, -a	separated
divorciado, -a	divorced
viudo, -a	widower, widow

Hijos *Sons and Daughters*

Él <u>tiene</u>...	He <u>has</u>...
Ella <u>tiene</u>...	She <u>has</u>...
un hij<u>o</u>, dos hij<u>os</u>	a son, two sons
una hij<u>a</u>, dos hij<u>as</u>	a daughter, two daughters
cuatro <u>hijos</u>	four children
El <u>no tiene</u> hijos.	He <u>does not have</u> children.
Ella <u>no tiene</u> hijos.	She <u>does not have</u> children.
<u>Ellos</u> <u>no</u> tien<u>en</u> hijos.	<u>They</u> <u>do not have</u> children.

Grammar in Use

Personal Pronouns

él (third person **masculine** personal pronoun)	he
ella (third person **feminine** personal pronoun)	she

Medical Specialties and Gender

Most nouns in Spanish show **masculine** gender when they **end in *o*** or in a **consonant preceded by *o*,** and they show **feminine** gender when they **end in *a*.** For example: *doct<u>or</u>, doctor<u>a</u>; cardiól<u>ogo</u>, cardiól<u>oga</u>; dermatól<u>ogo</u>, dermatól<u>oga</u>.*

As explained in Chapter 1, note that nouns ending in *-ista* and *-tra,* such as *nutricion<u>ista</u>, pedia<u>tra</u>,* and *obste<u>tra</u>,* have only one form and are used to refer to either a male or female professional. Other specialists in this group: *anestes<u>ista</u>* (anesthetist), *odontopedia<u>tra</u>* (pediatric dentist), *ortodonc<u>ista</u>* (orthodontist), *psiquia<u>tra</u>* (psychiatrist), *psicoanal<u>ista</u>* (psychoanalyst).

For more information about gender regarding health care professions, you can refer back to the Grammar in Use section in Chapter 1, page 3.

Verbs, Present Tense

trabajar   to work
trabaj<u>o</u> (first person singular)   I work
trabaj<u>a</u> (third person singular)   you (formal), he, she work(s)

> For example:
> **El Dr. Juan Luppi <u>trabaja</u> en el Hospital General, en Chile.**
> Dr. Luppi <u>works</u> at *Hospital General,* in Chile.

> More examples:
> **¿Dónde <u>trabaja</u> usted?**   Where <u>do you work</u>?
> **Yo <u>trabajo</u> en un supermercado.**   <u>I work</u> in a supermarket.

Refer back to Chapter 2, Vocabulary Practice section (Occupation and Place of Work), page 10, for more references and examples of the verb *trabajar.*

hablar   to speak
habl<u>o</u> (first person singular)   I speak
habl<u>a</u> (third person singular)   you (formal), he, she speak(s)

> For example:
> **La Dra. Akiko Sato <u>habla</u> japonés y español.**
> Dr. Akiko Sato <u>speaks</u> Japanese and Spanish.

> More examples:
> **¿Qué idiomas <u>habla</u> Joanna?**   What languages <u>does</u> Joanna <u>speak</u>?
> **Joanna <u>habla</u> español y portugués.**   Joanna <u>speaks</u> Spanish and Portuguese.

vivir   to live
viv<u>o</u> (first person singular)   I live
viv<u>e</u> (third person singular)   you (formal), he, she live(s)

> For example:
> **La Dra. Carmen Gutiérrez <u>vive</u> en Barcelona.**
> Dr. Carmen Gutiérrez <u>lives</u> in Barcelona.

> More examples:
> **¿Dónde <u>vive</u> usted?**   Where <u>do you live</u>?
> **Yo <u>vivo</u> en Barcelona.**   <u>I live</u> in Barcelona.
> **¿Dónde <u>vive</u> la Dra. Sato?**   Where <u>does</u> Dr. Sato <u>live</u>?
> **La Dra. Sato <u>vive</u> en Tokio.**   Dr. Sato <u>lives</u> in Tokyo.

You will find more information about verbs in the present tense in Appendix 2, Verb References, on page 137.

Adjectives Showing Marital Status

As with most adjectives, those showing marital status end in *o* for **masculine,** and in *a* for **feminine.**

> For example:
> **La Sra. María González es casad<u>a</u>.**
> **El Sr. José Pérez es casad<u>o</u>.**
> **El Sr. Martínez es divorciad<u>o</u>.**
> **Marta Gallegos es solter<u>a</u>.**

Sons and Daughters

In Spanish, when we refer to a general group, we use the masculine plural form of nouns as a way to generalize. If you want to be more specific about gender, you may want to use certain words that specify gender, such as when parents talk about their sons and daughters.

For **masculine** gender:
varón (boy, male child)
niño (boy, male child)

For **feminine** gender:
hembra (girl, female child)
niña (girl, female child)

For example:
¿Cuántos <u>hijos</u> tiene usted?
Tengo tres, un hij<u>o</u> y dos hij<u>as</u>.
Tengo tres, un niñ<u>o</u> y dos niñ<u>as</u>.
Tengo dos, un <u>varón</u> y una <u>hembra</u>.

How many children do you have?
I have three, a son and a daughter.
I have three, a boy and two girls.
I have two, a boy and a girl.

 ## Speaking Exercises

1. Listen to the dialog **"En una convención médica"** again (CD track 16). You will certainly have a great comprehension at this point! Then, go to page 35 and practice reading the dialog, changing the information about the people introduced.

2. Introduce the following health care professionals to an audience. Use the prompts below and remember to use the verbs in their third person singular forms: *es, vive, trabaja, habla, tiene, no tiene.*

   Pedro Palos / ginecólogo / Méjico / hospital en Veracruz / casado / tres hijos

   María Lovetto / cardióloga / Brasil / un hospital en Río de Janeiro / soltera

   Introduce other health care professionals you know to the same audience:

   Say his/her name: *El/Ella es...*

   Say his/her medical specialty: *El/Ella es...*

   Say where he/she lives: *El/Ella vive en...*

   Say where he/she works: *El/Ella trabaja en...*

   Say the languages he/she speaks: *El/Ella habla...*

3. Speak about yourself now! Use the prompts to answer. Notice that the verbs are now in the first person singular.

Provide your profession or occupation: *(Yo) Soy...*

Say where you live: *Vivo...*

Say where you work: *Trabajo...*

Say the languages that you speak: *Hablo...*

Give your marital status: *Soy...*

Tell how many children you have, if any: *Tengo.../No tengo...*

4. Read the following paragraph about Dr. Jim Díaz and answer the comprehension questions below. Additional information is provided to help you.

El Dr. Jim Díaz es pediatra. Vive en Miami, Florida. Él trabaja en un hospital en Coral Gables y además es profesor en la universidad. El Dr. Díaz también tiene pacientes particulares. Tiene dos consultorios médicos, uno en Miami Beach y otro en South Miami. Él es un excelente médico y una excelente persona.

Note the following words and structures:

Vive en Miami (with omitted subject)

además   besides
también   also, too

El Dr. Díaz también tiene pacientes particulares.
Dr. Díaz also has private patients.
Tiene dos consultorios médicos: uno en... y otro en...
He has two (medical) offices: one in... and another in...
El Dr. Díaz es un excelente médico y una excelente persona.
Dr. Díaz is an excellent doctor and an excellent person.

The indefinite article *un* matches with *médico:* masculine article, masculine noun. The indefinite article *una* matches with *persona:* feminine article, feminine noun.

Note the word order: *excelente médico*. In Spanish the noun generally comes first, then the adjective; but, when we want to provide extra emphasis to our description, we can invert the order.

COMPREHENSION QUESTIONS:

Find the following information in the paragraph about Dr. Jim Díaz. Answer in Spanish.

Where does Dr. Jim Díaz live?

What is his medical specialty?

What does he do apart from working in a hospital in Coral Gables?

How many offices does he have?

Where are his offices?

Is he a good professional?

Written Exercises

1. Write about Pedro Palos and María Lovetto, whom you introduced in Speaking Exercise 2. Refer back to that exercise if you need help with the use of verbs.

    Pedro Palos / ginecólogo / Méjico / hospital en Veracruz / casado / tres hijos

    María Lovetto / cardióloga / Brasil / un hospital en Río de Janeiro / soltera

    (a)_____

    (b)_____

2. Complete the following questions about Dr. Jim Díaz from Speaking Exercise 4.

    ¿Cuál es la especialidad médica del Dr. Díaz?

    El Dr. Díaz es (a)_____.

    ¿Dónde trabaja?

    Trabaja en un (b)_____, en (c)_____.

    ¿Tiene consultorios particulares? ¿Dónde?

    (d)_____

3. Write about two health care professionals you know. Complete the following information first, to use as a guide for your paragraphs. Refer back to Speaking Exercise 2 if you need some help when writing the paragraphs.

	Person A (male)	Person B (female)
Nombre:	_____	_____
Especialidad:	_____	_____
Lugar de trabajo:	_____	_____
Idiomas:	_____	_____
Estado civil:	_____	_____
Hijos:	_____	_____
Otra información:	_____	

Paragraph about person A:

_____

_____

_____

_____

Paragraph about person B:

_____

_____

_____

_____

4. Write a paragraph about yourself. Complete the following information first, to use as a guide for your paragraph. Refer back to Speaking Exercise 2 if you need some help when writing the paragraphs.

Nombre: _____

Ocupación: _____

Lugar de trabajo: _____

Idiomas: _____

Estado civil: _____

Hijos: _____

Otra información: _____

_____

_____

_____

_____

Role-Playing Exercise

En una convención médica *At a Medical Convention*

In the following situation, <u>you are a coordinator of activities</u> at an international medical meeting in Spain. There are health care professionals from all over the world. This is the first day, and participants are being introduced. Since there are both Spanish and English speakers in the audience, introductions are being made in both languages. Translate the following introductions for the Spanish speakers.

Good evening! We are going to make the introductions.

1. Dr. Juan Palacios is a cardiologist. He is from Italy. He lives in Rome. He works in two hospitals. He speaks Italian and Spanish.

2. Dr. Yugi Yasuo is a chiropractor. He is from Japan. He lives in Tokyo. He works in a chiropractic center. He speaks English and Japanese.

3. Dr. John Balt is a surgeon. He is from the United States. He lives in Miami, and he speaks English and Spanish. He works in a cosmetic surgery clinic in Miami Beach.

4. Dr. Melissa Green is an orthopedist. She is from England. She lives in London. She speaks English and German. She works in an orthopedic center, and she also has a private office.

5. Can you introduce some health care professionals you know?

Cultural Information

Many people from Spanish-speaking cultures are talkative and extroverted, and some like to share personal information and decisions with colleagues and work mates, no matter whether they have known each other for a short or a long time. They will sometimes ask some personal questions too, as a proof of concern for the other person, not in an attempt to interfere with someone's personal matters. This can sometimes cause misinterpretations, since a very extroverted person may perceive indifference on the part of another person who chooses not to ask about or prefers not to share information on a subject he or she regards as private. Of course, attitudes, choices, and considerations vary from person to person and may change with prolonged exposure to a certain cultural and social behavioral pattern.

Chapter 5

Haciendo una cita

Making an Appointment

In this chapter, you'll learn how to schedule appointments. You will learn how to schedule the month, day, and time of the appointment; how to spell names and last names; and how to ask for and provide any personal information required at a hospital admission desk or doctor's office. You will also be introduced to some cultural considerations regarding appointment scheduling.

Dialog: Necesito una cita con el doctor

I Need an Appointment with the Doctor

 La paciente Kem Khatkjial hace una cita con la secretaria de su dermatólogo.
Patient Kem Khatkjial makes an appointment with her dermatologist's secretary.

Secretaria:	**Buenas tardes.**
Paciente:	**Buenas tardes. Necesito una cita con el Dr. Gómez, por favor.**
Secretaria:	**Muy bien. ¿Para cuándo?**
Paciente:	**Para el miércoles por la tarde.**
Secretaria:	**Bien, hay un turno disponible a las cinco de la tarde.**
Paciente:	**Muy bien.**
Secretaria:	**¿Cuál es su nombre?**
Paciente:	**Kem Khatkjial.**
Secretaria:	**Por favor, ¿lo puede deletrear?**
Paciente:	**Sí, cómo no. Mi nombre es Kem: K-E-M y mi apellido Khatkjial: K-H-A-T-K-J-I-A-L.**
Secretaria:	**Bien, su número de teléfono por favor.**
Paciente:	**(953) 555-6790**
Secretaria:	**¿Edad?**
Paciente:	**Treinta y seis.**
Secretaria:	**¿Cuál es su seguro médico?**
Paciente:	**Medical Plan.**
Secretaria:	**¿Cuál es el motivo de la consulta?**
Paciente:	**Tengo una erupción, como una especie de acné.**
Secretaria:	**Muy bien, hasta el miércoles.**
Paciente:	**Muchas gracias, hasta el miércoles.**

Dialog Comprehension

Test your comprehension of the dialog by checking the correct options.

¿Cómo se llama la paciente?

Kem Khatkjial ☐

Gisella Gómez ☐

Juana Kelly ☐

Khatkjial es:

el nombre de la paciente ☐

el apellido de la paciente ☐

el teléfono de la paciente ☐

Medical Plan es:

la dirección de la paciente ☐

el seguro social de la paciente ☐

el seguro médico de la paciente ☐

Vocabulary Practice

In this section you will find words and phrases necessary for scheduling appointments.

Días de la semana *Days of the Week*

lunes	Monday	**viernes**	Friday
martes	Tuesday	**sábado**	Saturday
miércoles	Wednesday	**domingo**	Sunday
jueves	Thursday		

Unlike in English, the days of the week do not take capital letters in Spanish. The same concept applies to the months of the year.

Meses del año *Months of the Year*

enero	January	**julio**	July
febrero	February	**agosto**	August
marzo	March	**septiembre**	September
abril	April	**octubre**	October
mayo	May	**noviembre**	November
junio	June	**diciembre**	December

In many Spanish-speaking countries, the order of the date is written differently than in the United States. It is written as day/month/year. For example, in Spain one would say *el seis de noviembre* and write "6/11." Notice that the date is written in the same order as when it is spoken. Thus, and to avoid any misunderstandings, double check if in doubt!

Hora de la cita *Time of the Appointment*

¿Para cuándo?	(For) when?
<u>**Para** el...</u>	<u>For</u> (the)...
lunes	Monday
miércoles	Wednesday
4 de agosto	August 4th
Por la...	In the...(literally: during the)
mañana	morning
tarde	afternoon
noche	evening
A las...	At...
nueve de la mañana	nine in the morning
tres de la tarde	three in the afternoon
siete de la noche	seven in the evening

For example:
Necesito una cita <u>para el lunes</u> <u>por la mañana</u>.
I need an appointment <u>for Monday</u> <u>(in the) morning</u>.
Necesito una cita <u>para el viernes</u> <u>a las tres de la tarde</u>.
I need an appointment <u>for Friday</u> <u>at three in the afternoon</u>.

Please see Chapter 2 for more information on numbers, which will help to tell the time.

Averiguando la disponibilidad *Checking Availability*

Hay	There is, there are
¿Hay?	Is there...?/Are there...?

For example:
<u>Hay</u> un turno disponible a las cinco de la tarde.
<u>There is</u> an available space at 5 P.M.
<u>¿Hay</u> pacientes en la sala de espera?
<u>Are there</u> any patients in the waiting room?

Deletreando nombres *Spelling Names*

<u>¿Puede</u> deletrear su...	<u>Can you</u> spell your...
nombre?	name?
apellido?	last name?
<u>¿Lo</u> puede <u>deletrear</u>?	Can you <u>spell it</u>?

VOWELS

Vowel	Letter Name	As in...
A	ah	**alergia**
E	eh	**especialista**
I	eeh	**ibuprofeno**
O	oh	**ortopedista**
U	ooh	**urólogo**

CONSONANTS (LETTER + *EH*)

Consonant	Letter Name	As in...
B	beh	**biología**
C	seh	**cardiólogo, cerebro**
D	deh	**dermatólogo**
G	heh	**gastritis, gerontólogo**
P	peh	**pediatra**
T	teh	**tabletas**
V	beh	**vasectomía**

CONSONANTS (*EH* + LETTER + *EH*)

Consonant	Letter Name	As in...
F	ef-eh	**farmacia**
L	el-eh	**ligamento**
M	em-eh	**mamografía**
N	en-eh	**nitroglicerina**
Ñ	en-yeh	**baño**
R	er-eh	**radiografía**
S	es-eh	**suero**

CONSONANTS (MORE COMPLEX LETTER NAMES)

Consonant	Letter Name	As in...
H	ahcheh	**hueso**
J	hotah	**jarabe**
K	kah	**kilogramo**
Q	kuh	**queso**
W	doble-veh	**Walter**
X	ehkis	**rayo X**
Y	eeh-griega	**yeso**
Z	seta	**zoster**

Más números *More Numbers*

Refer to Chapter 2, page 9 to practice numbers 1 to 30. For numbers higher than 30, just add *y* (and).

For example:

31	**treinta y uno**
32	**treinta y dos**
33	**treinta y tres**

-nte, -nta		cien, -cientos		mil	
10	diez	100	**cien**	1000	**mil**
20	vei**nte**	200	dos**cientos**	2000	dos **mil**
30	trei**nta**	300	tres**cientos**	3000	tres **mil**
40	cuare**nta**	400	cuatro**cientos**	4000	cuatro **mil**
50	cincue**nta**	500	**quinientos**	5000	cinco **mil**
60	sese**nta**	600	seis**cientos**	6000	seis **mil**
70	sete**nta**	700	sete**cientos**	7000	siete **mil**
80	oche**nta**	800	ocho**cientos**	8000	ocho **mil**
90	nove**nta**	900	nove**cientos**	9000	nueve **mil**

...mil		...mil		...millón, -es	
10.000	diez **mil**	100.000	cien **mil**	1.000.000	un **millón**
20.000	veinte **mil**	200.000	doscientos **mil**	2.000.000	dos **millones**
30.000	treinta **mil**	300.000	trescientos **mil**	3.000.000	tres **millones**
40.000	cuarenta **mil**	400.000	cuatrocientos **mil**	4.000.000	cuatro **millones**
50.000	cincuenta **mil**	500.000	quinientos **mil**	5.000.000	cinco **millones**
60.000	sesenta **mil**	600.000	seiscientos **mil**	6.000.000	seis **millones**
70.000	setenta **mil**	700.000	setecientos **mil**	7.000.000	siete **millones**
80.000	ochenta **mil**	800.000	ochocientos **mil**	8.000.000	ocho **millones**
90.000	noventa **mil**	900.000	novecientos **mil**	9.000.000	nueve **millones**

1.000.000.000 is *mil millones,* commonly referred to as *billón,* although *mil millones* is the correct form. Unlike in English, in Spanish numbers greater than one thousand, use a period (.) not a comma (,).

Now that you have all the information about numbers, you only need to combine and practice them!

For example:

9	nueve
48	cuare**nta** y ocho
173	**ciento** sete**nta** y tres
6754	seis **mil** setecientos cincuenta y cuatro
38,032	treinta y ocho **mil** treinta y dos
223,251	dos**cientos** veintitrés **mil** dos**cientos** cincue**nta** y uno
4,673,295	cuatro **millones** seis**cientos** sete**nta** y tres **mil** dos**cientos** nove**nta** y cinco

Try to practice more numbers using the charts above!

La hora *Telling the Time*

	¿Qué hora es?	What time is it?
9:10	**Son las nueve y diez.**	It is nine ten.
9:15	**Son las nueve y quince.**	It is nine fifteen.
	Son las nueve y <u>cuarto</u>.	It is a <u>quarter past</u> nine.
9:20	**Son las nueve y veinte.**	It is nine twenty.
9:25	**Son las nueve y veinticinco.**	It is nine twenty-five.
9:30	**Son las nueve y treinta.**	It is nine thirty.
	Son las nueve y <u>media</u>.	It is <u>half past</u> nine.
9:40	**Son las nueve y cuarenta.**	It is nine forty.
	Son las diez <u>menos veinte</u>.	It is <u>twenty to</u> ten (literally, ten **minus** twenty)
9:45	**Son las nueve y cuarenta y cinco.**	It is nine forty-five.
	Son las diez <u>menos cuarto</u>.	It is a <u>quarter to</u> ten.

Grammar in Use

Prepositions

para	for	**a**	at
por	in, during	**de**	of, in

For example:
Necesito una cita <u>para</u> el lunes <u>por</u> la mañana.
I need an appointment <u>for</u> Monday in (<u>during</u>) the morning.
Necesito una cita <u>para</u> el miércoles <u>a</u> las tres <u>de</u> la tarde.
I need an appointment <u>for</u> Wednesday <u>at</u> three in (<u>of</u>) the morning.

Verbs

necesitar	to need
necesito (first person singular)	I need

For example:
<u>Necesito</u> una cita con el doctor.   <u>I need</u> an appointment with the doctor.

haber   impersonal verb for "to be"

In Spanish, the verb *hay* is used to say both "there is" and "there are." It is used both for singular and plural.

For example:
<u>Hay</u> un turno disponible a las tres de la tarde.   <u>There is</u> a space available at 3 P.M.

<u>Hay</u> dos pacientes en la sala de espera.   <u>There are</u> two patients in the waiting room.

poder   to be able to, can
puede (third person singular)   you (formal), he, she can

> For example:
> **¿Puede deletrear su apellido?**   <u>Can you</u> spell your last name?
> **¿Lo puede deletrear?**   <u>Can you</u> spell it?
> **¿Puede levantar el brazo?**   <u>Can you</u> raise your arm?

deletrear   to spell

> For example:
> **¿Lo puede <u>deletrear</u>?**   Can you <u>spell</u> it?

You will find more information on how verbs work in Appendix 2, Verb References, on page 137.

Telling the Time

Please note that, as distinct from English, in Spanish the time is given using the verb "to be" in its third person plural form *son*, except from **1:00 to 1:59,** where the singular verb *es* matches with the number *uno* "one." See also that the noun "time," *hora,* is feminine, thus we use *la* and *las* to refer to it, although numbers, except number one, remain unchanged. Let's keep it simple, observe differences, and keep practicing!

> For example:
> 1:00 <u>Es</u> la <u>una</u>.   1:20 <u>Es</u> la <u>una</u> y veinte.
>   It's one o'clock.   It's one twenty.
> 2:00 <u>Son</u> las <u>dos</u>.   2:30 <u>Son</u> las <u>dos</u> y media.
>   It's two o'clock.   It's two thirty.
> 4:00 <u>Son</u> las <u>cuatro</u>.   4:15 <u>Son</u> las <u>cuatro</u> y cuarto.
>   It's four.   It's a quarter past four.

 ## Speaking Exercises

1. Listen to the dialog **"Necesito una cita con el doctor"** again (CD track 19). You will see how easily you will understand it now. Then, go to page 46 and practice reading the dialog, changing the patient's information.

2. Using the Spanish alphabet, can you spell the following names?

   Miranda Jurado   Enrique Vélazquez

   Wilfredo Reyes   Begoña Mercury

3. Can you spell your name? *Por favor, ¿puede deletrear su nombre?*

4. Ask and answer about the following patients' ages.

Pacientes	Edades
Carla Rodríguez	34
Pedro Santos	58
Daniel Ordoñez	43
Juana Franco	29

For example:

¿Cuál es la edad de Carla Rodríguez?/¿Cuántos años tiene Carla Rodríguez?
Treinta y cuatro. Carla tiene treinta y cuatro años.

5. Practice asking someone his or her age. See the different ways you can ask the question, taking into account a more formal or informal situation:

To an elderly woman (using the "formal you"):
¿Cúantos años <u>tiene</u> <u>usted</u>?
Tengo cincuenta y ocho años.

To a child or young person (using the "informal you"):
¿Cúantos años <u>tienes</u> <u>tú</u>?
Tengo diez años.

Practice:

Ask Manuelita Galante, your new patient's little daughter.

You: ¿_____?

Manuelita: Siete.

Ask Delia Galante, your new patient's mother.

You: ¿_____?

Delia: Yo tengo sesenta y ocho años.

6. Practice saying the following numbers aloud.

32   110   57   6,900

7. Pretend you are recording an outgoing message in Spanish on your answering machine. The blank is to complete with your phone number:

Este es el _____, por favor, deje su mensaje después del tono. ¡Gracias!

This is _____, please leave a message after the tone. Thank you!

Extra Practice: Find a Spanish newspaper and look for articles or ads, search for numbers in them, and see if you can say them aloud, also trying to associate what those numbers represent. For example: *"...el 25 por ciento de las personas..."* means "...the 25 percent of the people..."; *"...1000 voluntarias en 32 hospitales..."* means "...1000 volunteers in 32 hospitals..." Are you ready to try? You may be amazed at how much you will be able to say and understand! You can refer back to the vocabulary section to check any numbers for help! You can use a dictionary to build your vocabulary while doing this exercise!

Written Exercises

1. Look at the chart with the patients' ages in Speaking Exercise 4. Complete the sentences below.

    ¿(a)_____ es la edad de Daniel Ordoñez?

    Cuarenta y tres.

    ¿Cuántos años tiene Pedro Santos?

    Pedro Santos tiene (b)_____ años.

    ¿(c)_____ es la (d)_____ de Juana Franco?

    Juana tiene veintinueve años.

    ¿Cuántos años tiene usted?

    Yo tengo _____ años.

2. Complete the questions or the answers. Write the complete numbers.

    Natalia   19   Luis   46   Carmen   67

    Pedro   24   Silvia   50   María   32

    For example:
    ¿Cuántos años tiene Natalia?
    Natalia tiene diecinueve años.

    ¿Cuántos años (a)_____ María?

    Maria tiene (b)_____.

    ¿(c)_____ Pedro?

    (d)_____ años.

    ¿(e)_____ Luis?

    (f)_____

¿(g)_____ Silvia?

(h)_____

¿(i)_____ Carmen?

(j)_____

3. Think of two people whose ages you know and write a sentence telling their ages.

_____

_____

4. Write some phone numbers you would like to practice in Spanish and check your spelling after writing them! You can try your cell phone, for example, or contact numbers you may need to provide.

_____ : _____

_____ : _____

_____ : _____

_____ : _____

_____ : _____

5. Following the example below, write the time at which you have your appointment.

   Secretaria: **¿A qué hora tiene cita con el doctor?**
   Patiente: **Tengo cita con el doctor a las cinco de la tarde.**

   2:00 P.M. (a)_____

   6:00 P.M. (b)_____

   9:00 A.M. (c)_____

   10:00 A.M. (d)_____

   7:00 P.M. (e)_____

6. Write out the times below:

   8:25 (a)_____   2:30 (d)_____

   7:40 (b)_____   1:15 (e)_____

   9:50 (c)_____   6:55 (f)_____

7. Write all the different ways to say the following times in Spanish.

Ask the question *"¿Qué hora es?"* first, then answer. Remember to use *es la una* to refer to one o'clock and *son las...* for all the numbers that show "more than one."

8:30

¿(a)_____?

(b)_____

(c)_____

10:15

¿(d)_____?

(e)_____

(f)_____

3:45

¿(g)_____?

(h)_____

(i)_____

1:30

¿(j)_____?

(k)_____

(l)_____

7:35

¿(m)_____?

(n)_____

(o)_____

8. The following information is about a general examination record that belongs to patient Leonardo Mares. Check any vocabulary you don't know in Appendix 1 at the back of the book.

> Informe: Chequeo general
> Nombre del paciente: Leonardo Mares
> Edad: 47 años
> Antecedentes: hipertensión, glucemia, resfríos y gripes frecuentes, cálculos en la vescícula

Esta es la agenda del paciente Mares para la semana próxima.
This is patient Mares's agenda for next week.

Horario	Lunes	Martes	Miércoles	Jueves	Viernes
7:30	análisis de sangre y orina				
8:15		radiografía de tórax			
8:30		electrocardio-grama			
10:00			resultado de los análisis		
12:00					
6:15				ecografía de vesícula	
7:20			Dr. Núñez, cardiólogo		Dr. Vázquez, médico general

Answer the following questions based on the information you have about him.

¿Cuántos años tiene el paciente Leonardo Mares?

(a) _____

¿Cuáles son sus antecedentes de salud?

(b) _____

¿Qué día va a hacerse los análisis de sangre y orina?

(c) _____

¿A qué hora tiene cita para su radiografía de tórax el martes?

(d)_____

¿Qué otro estudio va a realizarse el día martes?

(e)_____

¿Qué día tiene cita con el cardiólogo?

(f)_____

¿Cuándo va a tener el resultado de los análisis de sangre y orina?

(g)_____

¿Qué estudio va a realizarse el jueves?

(h)_____

¿Qué día y a qué hora tiene cita con el Dr. Vázquez?

(i)_____

¿Cuál es la especialidad médica del Dr. Vázquez?

(j)_____

Role-Playing Exercise

Haciendo una cita *Making an Appointment*

You will now have the opportunity of playing different roles.

SITUATION 1

<u>You are a patient</u>. You need an appointment with the doctor. You phone the doctor's office to schedule an appointment and provide the secretary with any required information.

SITUATION 2

<u>You play the part of a receptionist now</u>. Ask the patient for all the information you need to schedule an appointment (name, last name, telephone number, age, medical insurance, and chief complaint). Schedule the appointment.

SITUATION 3

<u>It is your turn to play the part of the doctor</u>. Take care of your patient.

SITUATION 1: MAKING THE APPOINTMENT

S: **Oficina del Dr. Palermo, buenas tardes.**
You: (Greet the secretary and say you need an appointment with Dr. Palermo.)
S: **Muy bien. ¿Para cuándo?**
You: (For Thursday morning.)
S: **Bien, hay un turno disponible a las nueve y diez de la mañana.**
You: (Ask if there is a space available at 10:00.)
S: **Sí, a las 10:00 está bien.**
You: (Say that is OK.)
S: **¿Cuál es su nombre?**
You: (Give your name)
S: **Por favor, ¿lo puede deletrear?**
You: (Spell your first and last name.)
S: **Bien, su número de teléfono por favor.**
You: (Give your phone number.)
S: **¿Edad?**
You: (Answer.)
S: **¿Cuál es su seguro médico?**
You: (Answer.)
S: **¿Cuál es el motivo de la consulta?**
You: (Pick a chief complaint for yourself.)
S: **Muy bien, hasta el jueves.**
You: (End the dialog.)

SITUATION 2: ASKING FOR THE PATIENT'S PERSONAL INFORMATION

You: (Ask the patient to say her name.)
P: **Soledad Paredes.**
You: (Ask what her address is.)
P: **3535 "NE" 210 calle.**
You: (Ask what her medical insurance is.)
P: **Mi seguro médico es "Vida saludable."**
You: (Ask her social security number.)
P: **Aquí tiene. Este es el número de mi seguro social.**
You: (Ask about her reason for visiting the office.)
P: **Hace días que siento mareos y tengo náuseas. Tengo también ardor en el estómago.**

SITUATION 3: TAKING CARE OF YOUR PATIENT

You: (Greet your patient, Mr. Estrada. It is 7 P.M.)
P: **Buenas noches.**
You: (Find out the patient's chief complaint.)
P: **Tengo dolores en los pies, en las piernas y en la espalda.**
You: (Ask how long he has had the pain.)
P: **Hace aproximadamente dos meses, pero ahora es muy fuerte.
      No puedo trabajar, doctor.**
You: (Ask him what his occupation is.)
P: **Soy pintor.**
You: (Tell him you are going to take an X-ray.)
P: **Bien, doctor.**
You: (Ask him if he is allergic to any medicine.)
P: **No, no soy alérgico a ninguna medicina.**

Cultural Information

Not all people consider preventive medicine a "need." Let's consider the quality of the foods most people tend to eat when in a hurry, as well as the high price of healthy foods such as fruits, vegetables, or meat, or the little exercise, if any, that time allows when work schedules are very busy. What about the expensive bill that may arrive for that "preventive consultation that might not be necessary"? Have you ever paid attention to what many kids eat every day? Sometimes, the visit to the doctor simply does not fit into time schedules if it is not "so necessary," not to mention a high number of Hispanic people without health insurance. There are many and different reasons to put off a visit to the doctor. Therefore, when a patient or patient's relative phones the doctor's office to schedule an appointment, there may be an urgent need. If no appointment is available, a "little space" for this "special consultation" will generally be pursued. In Latin countries doctors usually concede this space, since they plan in advance that they may have one or two unexpected patients per day.

Chapters 1 to 5 Self-Check Exercise

This is a good time to check your understanding and performance! Do the following exercises. You can check your answers in the Written Exercises Self-Check, Appendix 3, page 149.

1. Complete with the article *el* or *la,* as appropriate.

   (a)_____ paciente Eleonora Fernández tiene síntomas de apendicitis.

   (b)_____ Sr. González tiene dos hijas.

   (c)¿Qué día es _____ conferencia del Dr. Rodríguez?

   (d)Tengo una cita con _____ doctora Jiménez.

   (e) Mi cita es _____ jueves a las 9 de (f)_____ mañana.

2. Complete the dialogue with the appropriate question words.

   ¿Cuál?   **¿Cuánto?**   **¿Dónde?**   **¿Cuándo?**   **¿Qué?**

   ¿(a)_____ es su nombre?

   Manuel Torres Solá.

   ¿De (b)_____ es usted?

   Soy panameño.

   ¿(c)_____ hace que siente los mareos?

   Dos meses, aproximadamente.

   ¿(d)_____ tiene cita para los análisis de sangre y orina?

   El viernes a las ocho de la mañana.

   ¿Y (e)_____ día tiene cita con el doctor?

   El lunes.

3. Write the numbers.

365: (a)_____

4.500.000: (b)_____

1.800.000: (c)_____

30: (d)_____

2356: (e)_____

4. Translate into English.

enfermero: (a)_____

motivo: (b)_____

brazo izquierdo: (c)_____

cardióloga: (d)_____

consultorio médico: (e)_____

5. Translate into Spanish.

physician assistant: (a)_____

stomach: (b)_____

legs: (c)_____

doctor, physician: (d)_____

patient: (e)_____

6. Choose the correct verb form.

Yo (a)_____ el Doctor Martínez.	**es**	**soy**	**somos**
¿Dónde (b)_____ usted?	**trabajo**	**trabajan**	**trabaja**
Yo (c)_____ en Barcelona, España.	**vivo**	**vives**	**vivimos**
El paciente Soldán (d)_____ fiebre.	**tenemos**	**tiene**	**tengo**
El Sr. Pérez solamente (e)_____ español.	**hablo**	**hablas**	**habla**

Chapter 6

Indicando direcciones y expresando estados de ánimo

Giving Directions and Expressing Mood

In this chapter you will learn how to ask for and give directions. You will learn the different rooms and departments in a hospital, and the rooms in a house. You will also learn to express your own and other people's moods or states of mind.

Dialog: ¿Dónde está el laboratorio?

Where Is the Laboratory?

 La recepcionista del hospital está muy ocupada. El Sr. González necesita algunos datos, y el Dr. Martínez necesita hablar con el Dr. Torres.

The hospital receptionist is very busy. Mr. González needs some information and Dr. Martínez needs to talk to Dr. Torres.

Sr. González:	**Buenos días. Por favor, señorita, ¿dónde está el laboratorio?**
Recepcionista:	**El laboratorio está en el segundo piso, a la derecha.**
Sr. González:	**Muchas gracias. También necesito hacer una radiografía, ¿dónde está la sala de radiología?**
Recepcionista:	**Está al final del pasillo, a la izquierda. Al lado de la pediatría.**
Sr. González:	**Muy amable.**
Dr. Martínez:	**María, ¿dónde está el Dr. Torres?**
Recepcionista:	**El Dr. Torres está en la sala de partos. Doctor, ¿cómo está usted? Lo veo muy preocupado.**
Dr. Martínez:	**Sí, estoy preocupado. Necesito hablar con el Dr. Torres. Es urgente.**

Dialog Comprehension

Test your comprehension of the dialog by checking the correct options.

El paciente González necesita ir:

al laboratorio □

a la sala de emergencia □

a la sala de radiología □

El paciente González necesita hacerse:

una ecografía □

una radiografía □

una resonancia magnética □

La recepcionista se llama:

Juana □

María □

Susana □

Vocabulary Practice

In this section you will learn useful words and phrases necessary to ask for and give directions in a hospital setting. You will also learn how to refer to and describe states of mind or mood.

Ubicación de salas y de personas *Location of Rooms and People*

¿Dónde está el laboratorio?	Where is the laboratory?
Está en el primer piso, a la derecha.	It is on the first floor, on the right.
¿Dónde está la sala de radiología?	Where is the radiology room?
Está al final del pasillo, a la izquierda.	It is at the end of the corridor, on the left.
¿Dónde está el Dr. Torres?	Where is Dr. Torres?
Está en la sala de partos.	He is in the delivery room.

Salas y departamentos de un hospital *Rooms and Departments in a Hospital*

administración	administration
admisiones	admissions
sala de conferencias	conference room
sala de partos	delivery room
sala de emergencia	emergency room
sala de terapia intensiva	intensive care room

laboratorio	laboratory
sala de maternidad	maternity ward
medicina nuclear	nuclear medicine
nefrología	nephrology
terapia respiratoria	respiratory therapy
sala de cirugía	operating room
pediatría	pediatrics (department of)
sala de terapia física	physical therapy room
radiología	radiology
sala de rehabilitación	rehabilitation room
sala de reanimación	recovery room
sala de espera	waiting room
sala de ultrasonido	ultrasound room

Direcciones *Directions*

primer piso	first floor
segundo piso	second floor
tercer piso	third floor
enfrente de..., frente a...	across from...
al final del pasillo	at the end of the corridor
a su derecha	on your right
a su izquierda	on your left
hacia su derecha	to (toward) your right
hacia su izquierda	to (toward) your left
a la derecha de (los ascensores)	to the right of (the elevators)
a la izquierda de (los ascensores)	to the left of (the elevators)
arriba	upstairs
abajo	downstairs
al lado de (la cafetería)	next to (the cafeteria)

PISOS, NÚMEROS ORDINALES *Floors, Ordinal Numbers*

primero	first	sexto	sixth
segundo	second	séptimo	seventh
tercero	third	octavo	eighth
cuarto	fourth	noveno	ninth
quinto	fifth	décimo	tenth

Note that the first floor is *el prim**er** piso,* and the third floor, *el terc**er** piso.* After the tenth floor, the tendency is to keep it simple by saying just "floor 11." For example: *Piso 11, piso once; Piso 12, piso doce;* etc. A penthouse would be just *penthouse* or *último piso* (last floor). Also, some Spanish-speaking people would regard the first floor as *la planta baja,* which means "the ground floor," and some others would refer to "elevators" as *elevadores* rather than *ascensores.*

Estados de ánimo *States of Mind, Mood*

¿**Cómo** <u>está</u> (usted)?	<u>How are</u> you?
<u>Estoy</u> preocupado.	<u>I am</u> worried.
enojado, -a	annoyed
ansioso, -a	anxious
aburrido, -a	bored
ocupado, -a	busy
desilusionado, -a	disappointed
avergonzado, -a	embarrassed
entretenido, -a	entertained
asustado, -a	frightened
alegre	happy
feliz	happy
contento, -a	happy
hambriento, -a	hungry
enfermo, -a	ill
nervioso, -a	nervous
relajado, -a	relaxed
triste	sad
descompuesto, -a	sick

Grammar in Use

Verb *Estar*

Estar is another form of the verb "to be," thus it implies another way of saying "am," "is," or "are" in Spanish. *Estar* is the verb to be used when we refer to **location** of people and things and to **states of mind** or **mood**. As a general and main difference between the verbs *ser* and *estar*, we could say that *estar* is used in sentences showing mood, location, or temporal condition, while *ser* describes qualities, states, or conditions inherent to a person or thing. Compare for example:

La casa <u>es</u> grande.	The house <u>is</u> big. (*es*, inherent condition)
La casa <u>está</u> en la montaña.	The house <u>is</u> on the mountain. (*está*, location)
Ana <u>es</u> una persona feliz.	Ana <u>is</u> a happy person. (*es*, inherent condition)
Ana <u>está</u> feliz hoy.	Ana <u>is</u> happy today. (*está*, temporary condition)

SHOWING LOCATION

¿**Dónde** <u>está</u> el laboratorio?	Where <u>is</u> the laboratory?
<u>Está</u> al final del pasillo, a la derecha.	It <u>is</u> down the corridor, on the right.
El doctor Sánchez <u>está</u> en radiología.	Dr. Sanchez <u>is</u> in radiology.
La radiografía del paciente López <u>está</u> aquí.	The patient's X-ray <u>is</u> here.
La enfermera <u>está</u> en la sala de emergencias.	The nurse <u>is</u> in the emergency room.

SHOWING STATES OF MIND OR MOOD

¿Cómo <u>está</u> usted?	How <u>are</u> you?
<u>Estoy</u> muy preocupado.	I <u>am</u> very worried.
El paciente del Dr. Gómez <u>está</u> dolorido.	Dr. Gomez' patient <u>is</u> in pain.
El doctor Ramírez <u>está</u> preocupado.	Dr. Ramírez <u>is</u> worried.
La paciente Vargas <u>está</u> ansiosa.	Patient Vargas <u>is</u> anxious.

Note that adjectives are affected by gender. So, use the masculine form of adjectives for male and feminine for female.

For example:

<u>La</u> paciente <u>María</u> Juárez está descompuest<u>a</u>.	Patient María is sick.
Pedro está aburrid<u>o</u>.	Pedro is bored.

Please refer to Spanish Pronunciation and Grammar Basics on page xiv for more information about gender of adjectives.

 Speaking Exercises

1. Listen to the dialog **"¿Dónde está el laboratorio?"** again (CD track 22). Then read it aloud (page 63), changing either the locations asked for or directions given. You can visualize a medical building you know so that you can practice based on a real and meaningful setting.

2. Say where these people are and where the rooms are located.

Sra. Martínez	**sala de maternidad**	**3er piso**
Sr. Sánchez	**sala de emergencias**	**1er piso**
Dr. Torres	**sala de partos**	**2do piso**
Sra. Vásquez	**sala de espera**	**1er piso**
familia Prieto	**pediatría**	**2do piso**

For example:
La señora Martínez está en la sala de maternidad. La sala de maternidad está en el tercer piso.

3. Let's transfer the new structures to a new setting: home! Practice the following vocabulary items first:

Partes de la casa *Parts of the House*

altillo	attic	**jardín**	garden
sótano	basement	**cocina**	kitchen
dormitorio	bedroom	**garaje**	garage
baño	bathroom	**sala de estar**	living room
comedor	dining room	**sala de juegos**	playroom

The Bermúdez family is at home tonight. They are Mrs. and Mr. Bermúdez; Pedro, Susana, and Luis; María, the maid; Paco, their dog; and Michifuz, their cat. Where are they? How are they? Read the information and make up sentences in Spanish.

For example:
Pedro / living room / happy
Pedro está en la sala de estar. (Él) Está contento.

Can you now make up sentences with the following information? Look at the previous example for help, or refer back to the vocabulary section if needed.

Susana / bathroom / relaxed   María / kitchen / happy

Mrs. Bermúdez / bedroom / tired   Michifuz, the cat / basement / hungry

Mr. Bermúdez / garage / worried   Paco, the dog / garden / entertained

Eleonora / bedroom / bored   Luis / attic / happy

Extra Task: It would be a great practice to walk around your house or apartment while saying the names of the rooms aloud! Why don't you try?

Written Exercises

1. Answer these questions about Speaking Exercise 2. Try to provide complete answers to practice sentence construction.

    ¿Dónde está la Sra. Martínez?

    (a)_____

    ¿Dónde está la sala de emergencias?

    (b)_____

    ¿Dónde está la Sra. Vásquez?

    (c)_____

    ¿Dónde está la familia Prieto?

    (d)_____

    ¿Dónde está el departamento de pediatría?

    (e)_____

    ¿Dónde está la sala de espera?

    (f)_____

2. At home! Complete the questions by choosing the corresponding question word *Dónde* or *Cómo*. Read the replies as a guide for your choice.

¿(a)_____ está el Sr. Bermúdez?

Está en su dormitorio.

¿(b)_____ está Paco?

Está en el jardín.

¿ (c) _____ está Pedro?

Está contento.

¿(d)_____ está la Sra. Bermúdez?

Está relajada.

¿(e)_____ está Michifuz?

Está en el sótano.

¿(f)_____ está Luis?

Está contento.

¿(g)_____ está Eleonora?

Está en su dormitorio.

 Role-Playing Exercise

¿Dónde está la sala de rehabilitación? *Where Is the Rehabilitation Room?*

In the following situation patient Patricio Ramírez is at the hospital, as he needs to start his physical rehabilitation therapy. He has some trouble figuring out which direction to go. <u>You are a receptionist</u>. Imagine yourself at the reception desk of a health care facility you know and provide the patient with the directions he needs. Give as many details as possible for further practice.

P: **Disculpe, ¿Dónde está la sala de rehabilitación física?**
You: (Give directions.)
P: **Gracias. Y además tengo que hacerme una radiografía de tórax. ¿La sala de radiología está en el segundo piso?**
You: (Answer.)
P: **¿Y podría decirme también dónde hay un baño y dónde está la cafetería?**
You: (Answer.)
P: **Muchas gracias.**

Now listen to the dialog (CD track 25) between patient Ramírez and the rehabilitation therapist, and check your comprehension by answering the following questions:

Patient Ramírez is there to rehabilitate:

his right arm ☐

his left foot ☐

his left ankle ☐

He had:

a car accident ☐

an accident at work ☐

an accident in the street ☐

He works:

in construction ☐

in a school ☐

at a park ☐

He had:

surgery ☐

just a bandage ☐

a fracture and a cast ☐

He had the cast for:

six months ☐

seven weeks ☐

six weeks ☐

Chapter 7

La familia

The Family

In this chapter you will learn to introduce and talk about family members. You will also learn how to refer your patient to a specialist. You will find some cultural aspects regarding how relatives influence a patient's decision.

Dialog: Buenas tardes, doctor, él es mi marido

Good Afternoon, Doctor, This Is My Husband

 La Sra. María Lares tiene fuertes dolores de estómago todos los días después de comer. Ella va a ver a su médico general con su marido, el Sr. Juan Lares.
Mrs. María Lares has bad stomachaches every day after eating. She goes to see her general physician with her husband, Mr. Juan Lares.

Doctor:	**Buenas tardes.**
María:	**Buenas tardes, doctor.**
Doctor:	**Mucho gusto.**
María:	**Él es mi marido.**
Doctor:	**Mucho gusto, señor**
Juan:	**Mucho gusto, doctor.**
Doctor:	**Dígame, ¿qué la trae por aquí?, ¿en qué puedo servirle?**
María:	**Doctor, hace un tiempo tengo mucho dolor en el estómago.**
Juan:	**Sí, doctor. Ella tiene muchos dolores.**
Doctor:	**Y ¿cómo es el dolor?**
María:	**Bueno, es como un ardor. También tengo regurgitaciones y malestares.**
Doctor:	**Y ¿cuándo tiene más dolor?**
María:	**Generalmente después de comer.**
Doctor:	**Bien, veamos... Le voy a dar una orden para realizar unos análisis, y voy a referirla a un gastroenterólogo. Él le va a indicar estudios más específicos.**

Dialog Comprehension

Test your comprehension of the dialog by checking the correct options.

María has:

headaches	☐
pain in the legs	☐
stomachaches	☐

The general physician refers María to a:

gastroenterologist	☐
cardiologist	☐
nutritionist	☐

Vocabulary Practice

In this section you will learn vocabulary and phrases necessary to introduce family members. You will also learn ways to offer your patient help, and to refer him/her to a specialist.

Presentando a familiares *Introducing Family Members*

Él es...	He is...
Ella es...	She is...

For example:

Él es mi esposo.	He is my husband.
Ella es mi esposa.	She is my wife.

Los familiares *Family Members*

esposo, marido	husband
esposa	wife
hijo, -a	son, daughter
padre	father
madre	mother
suegro, -a	father-in-law, mother-in-law
hermano, -a	brother, sister
cuñado, -a	brother-in-law, sister-in-law
yerno	son-in-law
nuera	daughter-in-law
abuelo, -a	grandfather, grandmother
nieto, -a	grandson, granddaughter
bisabuelo, -a	great grandfather, great grandmother
bisnieto, -a	great grandson, great granddaughter
padrino	godfather
madrina	godmother
ahijado, -a	godson, goddaughter
tío, -a	uncle, aunt

sobrino, -a	nephew, niece
primo, -a	cousin
prometido, -a	fiancé, fianceé
cónyuge	spouse
novio, -a	boyfriend, girlfriend
amigo, -a	friend

Sometimes the words "parents" and "relatives" are mixed up when translated. "Parents" is *padres*, while "relatives" is *parientes* or *familiares.*

Recibiendo al paciente y ofreciéndole ayuda *Receiving the Patient and Offering Him/Her Help*

traer	to bring
servir	to serve
ayudar	to help
¿Qué <u>la/lo trae</u> por aquí?	What <u>brings you</u> up here?
¿En qué puedo <u>servirle</u>?	How can I <u>serve you</u>?
¿Cómo puedo <u>ayudarla/lo</u>?	How can I <u>help you</u>?

Derivando al paciente a un especialista *Referring the Patient to a Specialist*

referir	to refer
derivar	to refer
Voy a <u>referirla</u> a un especialista.	I am going to <u>refer you</u> (female) to a specialist.
Voy a <u>derivarlo</u> a un nutricionista.	I will <u>refer you</u> (male) to a nutritionist.

Please refer to Chapter 4, page 37, for specialists.

Grammar in Use

Brief Review of Possessive Adjectives *Mi* and *Su*

mi   my

For example:
Él es <u>mi</u> marido.   He is <u>my</u> husband.
Ella es <u>mi</u> suegra.   She is <u>my</u> mother-in-law.

su   your

For example:
¿Cómo está <u>su</u> marido?   How is <u>your</u> husband?
¿Cuál es <u>su</u> número de teléfono?   What is <u>your</u> phone number?

su   his, her

For example:
Mi nueva paciente se llama María Lares, y <u>su</u> marido siempre la acompaña.
My new patient's name is María Lares, and <u>her</u> husband always accompanies her.

Object Pronouns *La, Lo*

The object pronouns *la* and *lo* stand for "you" when it functions as a direct object of the verb. As you can see, some structures allow *lo* and *la* to be used either <u>before or after</u> the verb. When they come after the verb, pronoun and verb are written as one word. Please notice the use of *lo* when "you" is male, and the use of *la* when "you" is female.

For example :

Addressing a female patient:

Voy a referir<u>la</u> a un gastroenterólogo.	I will refer <u>you</u> to a gastroenterologist.
<u>La</u> voy a referir a un gastroenterólogo.	I will refer <u>you</u> to a gastroenterologist.

Addressing a male patient:

<u>Lo</u> voy a referir a un neurólogo.	I will refer <u>you</u> to a neurologist.
Tengo que referir<u>lo</u> a un cardiólogo.	I have to refer <u>you</u> to a cardiologist.

Object Pronoun *Le*

Le stands for "you" when it functions as indirect object of the verb. As in the case of *lo* and *la*, the object pronoun *le* can be placed before or after the verb. It is used to address either a male or female person.

For example:

Voy a dar<u>le</u> un calmante para el dolor.
I will give <u>you</u> a sedative for your pain.
Él <u>le</u> va a indicar un examen más completo.
He is going to indicate a more complete exam <u>to you</u>.
Voy a prescribir<u>le</u> una medicación.
I am going to prescribe <u>you</u> a medicine.

 ## Speaking Exercises

1. Listen to the dialog **"Buenas tardes, doctor, él es mi marido"** again (CD track 26). Then go to page 71 and read it, changing the family member that is being introduced each time you read.

2. Say the feminine of the following family members.

esposo	husband	**hijo**	son
padre	father	**padrino**	godfather
suegro	father-in-law	**tío**	uncle
hermano	brother	**nieto**	grandson
cuñado	brother-in-law	**ahijado**	godson
yerno	son-in-law	**abuelo**	grandfather
sobrino	nephew	**prometido**	fiancé

3. Practice referring the following patients to the specialists indicated below.

> For example:
> Mrs. Gonzalez, to a nutritionist
> **Sra. Gonzalez, la voy a derivar a un nutricionista.**

Now it's your turn!

Mr. Juárez, to a urologist

Mrs. Magdalena Fernandez, to an obstetrician

Mr. Luis Peña, to a psychologist

Mrs. Lorena Grant, to a gynecologist

Written Exercises

1. Three of your patients came to see you today, accompanied by a relative. Write as in the following example:

> Patient María came with Juan, her husband.
> **Mi paciente se llama María. Su esposo se llama Juan.**

Patient Manuel Cadenas came with Delia, his wife.

Patient Beatriz Contreras came with Mauricio, her son.

Patient Carlos Valler came with Eugenia, his mother.

Now write about them as in the example:

(a)_____

(b)_____

(c)_____

2. Complete with the corresponding possessive pronoun: *su* or *mi*.

¿Cómo le va, doctor? Le presento a (a)_____ hermana.

La paciente María Gómez está en el consultorio con (b)_____ madre.

(c)_____ abuela y yo hablamos por teléfono todos los viernes.

José visita a (d)_____ familia todas las semanas.

(e)_____ cuñado, el marido de mi hermana, habla inglés, italiano y español.

3. Complete with the objective pronoun that corresponds: *lo* or *la.*

> Señor Soldán, (a)_____ voy a derivar a un neurólogo.

> Señor Gómez, tengo que derivar (b) _____ a un nutricionista.

> Señorita Díaz, (c) _____ vamos a derivar a un endocrinólogo.

> Señora Gutiérrez, vamos a derivar (d) _____ a un obstetra.

> Señor Martínez, tengo que derivar (e) _____ a un urólogo.

4. Find and circle the indirect object pronoun *le* in all the sentences, and then translate the sentences.

> Sr. Gonzalez, voy a prescribirle un jarabe para la tos.

> (a)_____

> Sra. Pérez, el nutricionista le indicará una dieta.

> (b)_____

> Sr. Ramírez, voy a prescribirle una medicina para su dolor.

> (c)_____

> Sra. Suárez, vamos a hacerle una radiografía de la cadera.

> (d)_____

5. Match each Spanish word to its English translation. The first one is done for you.

novia	sister
suegra	friend
amigo	daughter
cuñado	mother-in-law
madre	niece
hermana	girlfriend
abuela	nephew
hija	brother-in-law
sobrino	mother
sobrina	grandmother

6. Think of family members and write a sentence about each of them. You can write about each person's name, age, nationality, place of work, marital status, children, place of residence, languages spoken, etc. Let's revisit the conjugation of the third person singular for some common verbs you might need: *es, tiene, vive, trabaja, habla.* For additional help with verbs, please go to the Verb Reference section, page 137.

> For example:
> **Mi hermana vive en Italia. Trabaja en una escuela de arte en Roma.**
> **Mi sobrino habla italiano, español e inglés.**

_____

_____

_____

_____

_____

Role-Playing Exercise

La familia *The Family*

In the following situation <u>you are a general physician</u>. Patient Franco Cascos comes to your office with his wife, Bianca Cascos. Deal with the patient's chief complaint, as well as with his wife's comments. You will need to refer your patient to a specialist.

You:	(Greet your patient. It's 6:00 P.M.)
P:	**Buenas tardes, doctor. Le presento a mi esposa, Bianca.**
You:	(Respond.)
B:	**Mucho gusto, doctor.**
You:	(Ask patient what brings him to your office.)
P:	**Doctor, hace un tiempo tengo muchos dolores musculares, me duele mucho la espalda, los brazos y el cuello.**
B:	**Sí, doctor. Estoy muy preocupada. A veces no puede mover el cuello. Tiene mucho dolor.**
You:	(Ask the patient when he has more pain.)
P:	**Tengo más dolor por la noche.**
You:	(Ask the patient if he takes any medicine for pain.)
P:	**No, no tomo ninguna medicina.**
B:	**Doctor, aquí tenemos la radiografía que nos dió el médico de emergencias.**
You:	**A ver, bien.**
P:	**¿Y, doctor?**
You:	(Refer the patient to an orthopedist.)
B:	**Muy bien doctor. Vamos a hacer una cita con un ortopedista, entonces.**

Cultural Information

It is very common to have a patient who comes to consult you accompanied by a relative. Relatives will very probably be as much or even more involved in the situation than the patient himself or herself. It will be very important to make the relative feel comfortable and keep him or her well informed, since the patient will often rely on this relative for further visits to your office or attitudes toward any treatments you indicate.

<table>
<tr><td>

Chapter 8

</td><td>

¿Cómo es el paciente físicamente?

</td></tr>
</table>

What Does the Patient Look Like?

In this chapter you will learn how to describe people physically and refer to what they are doing. You will also learn to talk about the weather.

Dialog: ¿Cómo es el Sr. Pérez?

What Does Mr. Pérez Look Like?

 La enfermera Rodríguez no conoce al paciente Pérez.
Nurse Rodríguez does not know patient Pérez.

Doctor:	**¡José Pérez!... ¡José Pérez!... ¿Dónde está el paciente Pérez?**
Enfermera:	**Doctor, ¿cómo es el Sr. Pérez?**
Doctor:	**Es un señor de mediana edad. Es alto, tiene cabello castaño, tez morena y ojos marrones.**
Enfermera:	**Bien. Doctor, ¿el paciente Pérez es ese señor que está tomando agua?**
Doctor:	**Sí. Es él. Gracias, enfermera. Señor Pérez, ¡adelante!**
Sr. Pérez:	**Oh, sí doctor. Estoy tomando agua fresca, hace mucho calor aquí, ¿verdad?**
Doctor:	**Sí, es verdad, tiene razón. Hace calor.**
Enfermera:	**Doctor, ¿vio al Dr. Céspedes?**
Doctor:	**Sí. Está en la sala de radiografías. Está conversando con el radiólogo.**
Enfermera:	**Gracias doctor.**

Dialog Comprehension

Test your comprehension of the dialog by checking the correct options.

¿Cuál es el apellido del paciente?
Pérez ☐
Fernández ☐
Rodríguez ☐

¿Dónde está el Sr. Pérez?
en su casa ☐
en su trabajo ☐
en el hospital ☐

¿Dónde está el Dr. Céspedes?
en su casa ☐
en su trabajo ☐
en el hospital ☐

Vocabulary Practice

In this section you will learn a lot of vocabulary to describe people. You will also learn vocabulary to describe the weather.

Describiendo a una persona físicamente *Describing a Person Physically*

¿Cómo es el, la paciente?	What does the patient look like?
Él, Ella es...	He, She <u>is</u>...
Él, Ella tiene...	He, She <u>has</u>...

Referencias de edad *Age References*

Él, Ella es un niño, una niña.	He, She <u>is</u> a child.
un, una adolescente	an adolescent
una persona joven	a young person
una persona de mediana edad	a middle-aged person
una persona mayor	an elderly person
una persona anciana	an old person

Tez *Complexion*

Él, Ella tiene tez blanca.	He, She <u>has</u> a white complexion.
negra	black
clara	fair
oscura	dark
bronceada	tanned
trigueña	light brown, olive
morena	brown

Estatura *Height*

Él, Ella es alto, -a.	He, She is tall.
bajo, -a	short
de mediana estatura	medium height

Contextura física *Build*

Él, Ella es delgado, -a.	He, She is thin.
gordo, -a	fat
de contextura pequeña	of small build
de contextura mediana	of medium build
de contextura grande	of large build

Cabello *Hair*

Él, Ella tiene cabello rubio.	He, She has blond hair.
claro	fair
oscuro	dark
negro	black
marrón	brown
castaño	chestnut
pelirrojo	red
canoso, con canas	gray
largo	long
corto	short
lacio	straight
ondeado	wavy
enrulado	curly
crespo	frizzy

Ojos *Eyes*

Él, Ella tiene ojos azules.	He, She has blue eyes.
verdes	green
marrones	brown
castaños	light brown
grises	gray

Otros *Other Features*

barba	beard	pestañas	eyelashes
hoyuelos	dimples	anteojos, lentes	glasses
cejas (gruesas, finas)	eyebrows (thick, thin)	bigotes	mustache

Describiendo lo que hace una persona *Describing What a Person is Doing*

El señor **está** tom**ando** agua.	The man <u>is</u> drink<u>ing</u> water.
El médico **está conversando** con el radiólogo.	The doctor <u>is</u> talk<u>ing</u> to the radiologist.
El paciente **está** com**iendo**.	The patient <u>is</u> eat<u>ing</u>.

You can also describe someone in terms of what they are doing using relative clauses. For example:

El Sr. Pérez es el señor <u>que está tomando agua</u>.
Mr. Pérez is the man <u>who is drinking water</u>.
Él es el médico <u>que está atendiendo a mi abuela</u>.
He is the doctor <u>who is taking care of my grandmother</u>.

Conversando acerca del tiempo *Talking About the Weather*

¿Cómo está el tiempo?	What's the weather like?
¿Qué tiempo hace?	What's the weather like?
	(literally: What weather does it make?)
Hace calor.	It is hot.
frío	cold
Está soleado.	It is sunny.
nublado	cloudy
lluvioso	rainy
nevando	snowing
lloviendo	raining
ventoso	windy
Hay...	There is...; There are...
nubes	clouds
rocío	dew
niebla	fog
nieve	snow
sol	sun
viento	wind

Grammar in Use

Asking Questions with *Cómo*

¿Cómo?	How? (What?)

For example:
<u>¿Cómo</u> es el Sr. Pérez?   <u>What</u> does Mr. Pérez look like?

Notice the difference betweeen the questions *¿Cómo <u>es</u> el Sr. Pérez?* and *¿Cómo <u>está</u> el Sr. Pérez?* In the first question we want to know his physical appearance, what he looks like; while in the second one, we want to know how he feels. If you need to, refer back to Chapter 6, page 66, to revisit how to ask about a person's state of mind or mood.

Agreement in Number and Gender Between Adjective and Noun

Remember that nouns and adjectives agree in number and gender. You can revisit the Spanish Pronunciation and Grammar Basics section (page xiv) and Chapter 2 (page 7) to review this topic. As a general rule, remember that most nouns and adjectives ending in *a* are feminine, and those ending in *o* are masculine.

For example:

Ella tiene cabe<u>llo</u> oscu<u>ro</u>. She has dark hair.
Él tiene ce<u>jas</u> grue<u>sas</u>. He has thick eyebrows.

Adjectives such as *marró<u>n</u>* (brown), *azu<u>l</u>* (blue), *jove<u>n</u>* (young), ending in a consonant letter, or those ending in *e*, such as *verd<u>e</u>* (green), or *inteligent<u>e</u>* (intelligent), remain unchanged for masculine or feminine. In some nouns such as *tez*, gender is difficult to recognize. Dictionaries specify the gender of all words.

The Present Progressive Tense

The present progressive tense describes actions happening <u>now</u>. As we know, in English it is made up by the conjugated form of the verb "to be" plus the main verb ending in **-ing.** In Spanish it is very similar, and thus we have the conjugated form of the verb "to be," *estar,* plus the main verb ending in **-*ando* or -*iendo*.**

For example:

El médico <u>está</u> examin<u>ando</u> al paciente. The doctor <u>is</u> examin<u>ing</u> the patient.
La enfermera <u>está</u> ayud<u>ando</u> al paciente. The nurse <u>is</u> help<u>ing</u> the patient.
El cardiólogo <u>está</u> auscult<u>ando</u> al paciente. The cardiologist <u>is</u> auscultat<u>ing</u> the patient.
El paciente <u>está</u> tom<u>ando</u> agua. The patient <u>is</u> drink<u>ing</u> water.
La Sra. Díaz <u>está</u> camin<u>ando</u> en el parque. Mrs. Díaz <u>is</u> walk<u>ing</u> in the park.
El paciente Helguera <u>está</u> com<u>iendo</u> mejor. Patient Helguera <u>is</u> eat<u>ing</u> better.

RELATIVE CLAUSES WITH A VERB IN THE PRESENT PROGRESSIVE

When we want to describe someone in terms of what he or she is doing, the verb is within the relative or adjectival clause, which qualifies the noun. The relative clause is introduced by *que* (that), meaning "that" or "who."

For example:

El paciente López es el señor <u>que está tomando agua</u>.
Patient López is the man <u>who is drinking water</u>.
Mi hijo es el niño <u>que está comiendo un sándwich</u>.
My son is the boy <u>who is eating a sandwich</u>.
María Céspedes es la señora <u>que está leyendo un libro</u>.
María Céspedes is the lady <u>who is reading a book</u>.

Speaking Exercises

1. Listen to the dialog "**¿Cómo es el Sr. Pérez?**" again (CD track 29). Then go to page 79 and read it aloud, changing the patients and their physical descriptions, and the actions carried out by them.

2. Practice different descriptions of people until you become fluent and can handle all the vocabulary. Then, think of a person you know or a well-known person. You will be asked questions regarding his or her physical appearance on the CD; answer *Sí...* or *No...*

    Play the CD track (30). You can do this activity as many times as you like, thinking of different people each time, to practice different vocabulary.

    Think of a female person first. Ready? Now listen to the questions on the CD and answer *Sí* or *No.*

    Think of a male person now. Ready? Now listen to the questions on the CD and, again, answer *Sí* or *No.*

3. Look around. Find objects you can use and pretend you are doing something. For example, pick up a bottle of water to pretend you are drinking water, a pen to pretend you are writing, a book to pretend you are reading. Also, look for people doing different activities around you and describe what they are doing. Remember to use *estoy* when you speak about yourself, and *está* when you refer to someone else.

    For example:
    Yo estoy tomando agua.   **El señor está caminando.**

    Look at the following verbs in their *-ando, -iendo* forms.

tomar	drink, take	**estoy, está tomando**
beber	drink	**estoy, está bebiendo**
manejar	drive	**estoy, está manejando**
comer	eat	**estoy, está comiendo**
buscar	look for	**estoy, está buscando**
leer	read	**estoy, está leyendo**
estudiar	study	**estoy, está estudiando**
caminar	walk	**estoy, está caminando**
escribir	write	**estoy, está escribiendo**

4. Look outside and answer the following question about the weather. Give as much information as possible.

    ¿Cómo está el tiempo?

Written Exercises

1. Write a paragraph about one male and one female person you picked while doing Speaking Exercise 2.

    Remember!

    Él, Ella es...   He, She is...
    Él, Ella tiene...   He, She has...

Female:

_____

_____

_____

Male:

_____

_____

_____

2. Complete with *es* or *tiene*.

María (a)_____ alta y delgada. Ella (b)_____

ojos azules y tez clara.

El Dr. Fuentes (c)_____ alto y (d)_____

cabello negro con canas. (e)_____ tez trigueña y ojos marrones.

El paciente Ramírez (f)_____ de mediana edad. Él

(g)_____ muy alto, y (h)_____ ojos

marrones y cabello castaño y ondeado.

3. Can you write a paragraph describing a favorite celebrity physically? Here you have some guidelines to start the paragraph.

Mi ... favorito, -a es ...

Useful words:

actor	actor	**futbolista**	soccer player
actriz	actress	**tenista**	tennis player
cantante	singer	**escritor, -a**	writer

_____

_____

_____

_____

_____

Role-Playing Exercise

¿Cómo es su paciente? *What Does Your Patient Look Like?*

In the following situation <u>you are a doctor</u> working in a hospital. In the different dialogs you are looking for various patients you have to see. You provide the nurse with a general physical description of your patient so that she can look for him/her. Try to think of real people, and your practice will be more meaningful to you. Please refer to the vocabulary section for any words you don't remember, and incorporate them into your descriptions. Notice that when the nurse says "*Ya voy a buscarlo/la*" she is saying "I am going to look for him/her right now."

Situation 1: Think of a male patient.

Enfermera: **¿Y cómo es su paciente, doctor?**

You: _____

Enfermera: **Bien, doctor, ya voy a buscarlo.**

Situation 2: Think of a female patient.

Enfermera: **¿Y cómo es su paciente, doctor?**

You: _____

Enfermera: **Bien, doctor, ya voy a buscarla.**

Situation 3: Think of a male child.

Enfermera: **¿Y cómo es su paciente, doctor?**

You: _____

Enfermera: **Bien, doctor, ya voy a buscarlo.**

Situation 4: Think of a female adolescent.

Enfermera: **¿Y cómo es su paciente, doctor?**

You: _____

Enfermera: **Bien, doctor, ya voy a buscarla.**

Chapter 9

¿Cuándo tiene más dolor?

When Do You Have More Pain?

In this chapter you will learn to ask your patient questions regarding his or her previous visit to your office. You will also learn to ask at what times of the day he or she is in more pain, and you will be able to give more precise indications about what time medicines should be taken.

Dialog: Sigo con dolores en los pies

I Still Have Pains in My Feet

 El paciente Gerardo García realiza su segunda visita al centro ortopédico.
Patient Gerardo García goes to the orthopedic center for a second time.

Doctor:	**¿Cómo está, Sr. García? ¿Cómo se siente?**
Sr. García:	**Regular, un poco dolorido.**
Doctor:	**¿Qué le pasa?**
Sr. García:	**Sigo con mucho dolor en los pies, en las plantas de los pies y en los tobillos.**
Doctor:	**A ver, cuénteme. ¿Dónde es el dolor exactamente?**
Sr. García:	**Aquí, y aquí.**
Doctor:	**¿Y cuándo tiene más dolor?**
Sr. García:	**Por la madrugada, cuando me levanto.**
Doctor:	**Y ¿durante el día?**
Sr. García:	**A veces, cuando camino mucho, o después de hacer mucho ejercicio, pero no puedo jugar al fútbol.**
Doctor:	**¿Tomó el antiinflamatorio que le di?**
Sr. García:	**Sí, doctor. Tomé el antiinflamatorio como usted me indicó.**
Doctor:	**Bien. Vamos a hacer otra radiografía.**

Después de la radiografía

Doctor:	**Vamos a cambiar la dosis de la medicación. Tome el antiinflamatorio con las comidas principales, uno con el almuerzo y otro con la cena durante dos semanas. Haga vida normal, pero no haga ejercicio por estas semanas. Vamos a ver cómo evoluciona. Si no mejora voy a referirlo a un especialista en podiatría.**

Dialog Comprehension

Test your comprehension of the dialog by checking the correct options.

¿Dónde tiene dolor el Sr. García?

en el pecho ☐

en los pies ☐

en las rodillas ☐

¿Es esta la primera visita del Sr. Pérez al centro ortopédico?

sí ☐

no ☐

What do you think the doctor prescribed?

a different medicine ☐

a new anti-inflammatory ☐

a different dose of the same anti-inflammatory ☐

Vocabulary Practice

In this section you will find words and phrases necessary to follow up with your patient.

Preguntando cómo está el paciente *Asking How the Patient Is Doing*

¿Cómo está?	How are you?
¿Cómo se siente?	How do you feel?
Muy bien, gracias.	Very well, thanks.
Bien.	Fine.
Regular.	Not bad.
Más o menos; Así, así.	So-so.
Mal.	Bad.
Muy dolorido.	In pain.
Sigo con dolores.	I still have pain.

Expresando dolor *Expressing Pain*

Me <u>duele</u> mucho el, la...	My (body part, singular) <u>hurts</u> a lot.
Me <u>duelen</u> mucho los, las...	My (body parts, plural) <u>hurt</u> a lot.

For example:

Me <u>duele</u> mucho el abdomen.	My abdomen <u>hurts</u> a lot.
Me <u>duele</u> mucho la cabeza.	My head <u>hurts</u> a lot.
Me <u>duelen</u> mucho los tobillos.	My ankles <u>hurt</u> a lot.
Me <u>duelen</u> mucho las mamas.	My breasts <u>hurt</u> a lot.

Más partes del cuerpo *More Parts of the Body*

el abdomen	the abdomen
el tobillo, los tobillos	the ankle, the ankles
la axila, las axilas	the armpit, the armpits
la mama, el seno, las mamas, los senos	the breast, breasts
el codo, los codos	the elbow, the elbows
la cara	the face
la articulación, las articulaciones	the joint, the joints
la pierna, las piernas	the leg, the legs
la nuca	the nape (of the neck)
el ombligo	the navel
el cuello	the neck
la palma, las palmas (de las manos)	the palm, the palms (of the hands)
la planta, las plantas (de los pies)	the sole, the soles (of the feet)
la cintura	the waist
la muñeca, las muñecas	the wrist, the wrists

Más vocabulario relativo a medicinas *More Vocabulary Regarding Medicines*

antiinflamatorio	anti-inflammatory
loción para picazones o prurito	anti-itch lotion
pastillas anticonceptivas	contraceptive pills
laxante	laxative
crema para dolores musculares	muscle pain ointment
descongestivo nasal	nasal decongestant
parche	patch
calmante	sedative

Averiguando cuándo el paciente tiene más dolor *Finding Out When the Patient Has More Pain*

¿Cuándo tiene <u>más</u> dolor?	When do you have <u>more</u> pain?

MOMENTOS DEL DÍA *Times of Day*

a la madrugada	very early in the morning
a la mañana	in the morning
al mediodía	at midday
a la tarde	in the afternoon
a la noche	at night

MIENTRAS REALIZA CIERTAS ACTIVIDADES *While Doing Certain Activities*

Cuando me levanto	When I get up
me acuesto	lie down
me siento	sit down
me paro	stand up
me ducho	take a shower
me visto	get dressed
camino	walk
leo	read
toso	cough
manejo	drive
hago ejercicio	exercise
levanto peso	lift weight

For example:
Tengo mucho dolor <u>a la mañana</u> <u>cuando me levanto</u>.
I have a lot of pain <u>in the morning</u> <u>when I get up</u>.
Me duele mucho la cabeza <u>a la noche</u> <u>cuando me acuesto</u>.
My head hurts a lot <u>in the evening</u> <u>when I go to bed</u>.
Me duele mucho la muñeca <u>cuando me visto</u>.
My wrist hurts a lot <u>when I get dressed</u>.

Hablando acerca de lo que el paciente puede y no puede hacer *Talking About What the Patient Can and Cannot Do*

<u>**No puedo**</u> **jugar al fútbol.**	<u>I can't</u> play soccer.
jugar al tenis	play tennis
hacer ejercicio	exercise
caminar mucho	walk for long
¿<u>**Puede**</u> **mover el pie?**	<u>Can you</u> move your foot?
dormir de noche	sleep at night
extender el brazo	extend your arm
Sí, <u>puedo</u>. / No, <u>no puedo</u>.	Yes, <u>I can</u>. / No, <u>I can't</u>.

Note that *fútbol* is the Spanish word for "soccer." Some people in Spanish-speaking countries have begun to say "soccer," although it is not recognized as a Spanish word. "Football" as understood in the United States would be specified as *fútbol americano* in Spanish.

Preguntas acerca de la visita anterior *Questions Regarding the Previous Visit*

¿<u>**Tomó**</u> **la medicina <u>que le di</u>?**	<u>Did you take</u> the medicine <u>that I gave you</u>?
¿<u>**Tomó**</u> **el antiinflamatorio <u>que le prescribí</u>?**	<u>Did you take</u> the anti-inflammatory <u>that I prescribed you</u>?
¿<u>**Tomó**</u> **los analgésicos <u>que le di</u>?**	<u>Did you take</u> the analgesics <u>that I gave you</u>?

Indicando como tomar la medicina *Indicating How to Take Medicine*

Tome la medicina <u>después</u> de las comidas.	Take the medicine <u>after</u> meals.
<u>antes</u> de las comidas	<u>before</u> meals
<u>entre</u> comidas	<u>between</u> meals
<u>con</u> las comidas	<u>with</u> meals
Tome una píldora <u>por día.</u>	Take one pill <u>per day.</u>
Tome un comprimido <u>cada</u> seis horas.	Take one pill <u>every</u> six hours.
Vamos a <u>cambiar</u> la dosis.	We are going to <u>change</u> the dose.
Vamos a <u>reforzar</u> la dosis.	We are going to <u>increase</u> the dose.

Grammar in Use

Present Tense Verbs

seguir (irregular verb)	to continue, to go on
Sigo con...	I continue, I go on with...

For example:

Todavía <u>sigo con</u> dolores y molestias.	I <u>still have</u> pains and discomforts.
<u>Vamos a seguir</u> con este tratamiento.	<u>We are going to continue</u> with this treatment.

doler (irregular verb)	to hurt
duele	it hurts (third person singular)
duelen	they hurt (third person plural)

We say *me duele...* when only one part of the body hurts. We say *me duelen...* when two or more parts of the body hurt. Note that *me* functions as an object pronoun. As you can see, in these examples the object pronoun *me* corresponds to "me."

For example:

Me <u>duele</u> la cabeza.	My head <u>hurts</u> (me).
Me <u>duelen</u> las piernas.	My legs <u>hurt</u> (me).

Reflexive Verbs

The infinitive forms of reflexive verbs in Spanish consist of the main verb plus the reflexive pronoun *se.* A verb is reflexive when the subject and the object are the same.

levantar(se)	to get (oneself) up	**parar(se)**	to stand (oneself) up
acostar(se)	to lie (oneself) down	**duchar(se)**	to shower (oneself)
sentar(se)	to sit (oneself) down	**vestir(se)**	to get (oneself) dressed

The <u>reflexive pronoun</u> refers to the person who receives the action of the verb. The pronoun that corresponds to the first person *yo* is *me.*

Cuando (yo) <u>me</u> levanto	When I get up
me acuesto	I lie down
me siento	I sit down
me paro	I stand up
me ducho	I take a shower
me visto	I get dressed

For example:
Yo me levanto a las siete de la mañana todos los días.
I get up at seven o'clock every morning.
Generalmente, me acuesto muy tarde.
In general, I go to bed very late.

You will find more information about reflexive verbs in Chapter 3, page 28, and in Chapter 10, page 105.

Past Tense Verbs

tomar	to take
tomé (first person singular)	I took
tomó (third person singular)	you (formal), he, she took

For example:
¿Tomó los antibióticos?   Did you take the antibiotics?
Sí, doctor, tomé los antibióticos.   Yes, doctor, I took the antibiotics.
Tomé la medicina después del almuerzo.   I took the medicine after lunch.
¿A qué hora tomó el analgésico?   At what time did you take the analgesic?

dar (irregular verb)	to give
di (first person singular)	I gave
dio (third person singular)	you (formal), he, she gave

For example:
Ya le di el calmante al paciente García.   I already gave the sedative to patient García.
Le di la prescripción a su hijo.   I gave the prescription to your son.
El doctor me dio estas píldoras.   The doctor gave me these pills.

prescribir	to prescribe
prescribí (first person singular)	I prescribed
prescribió (third person singular)	you (formal), he, she prescribed

For example:
¿Tomó los calmantes que le prescribí?   Did you take the sedatives I prescribed you?
Le prescribí un antibiótico.   I prescribed you an antibiotic.

Demonstrative Adjectives: *este, esta, estos, estas*

Demonstrative adjectives in Spanish agree in gender and number with the noun.

this	these
este (masculine) **esta** (feminine)	**estos** (masculine) **estas** (feminine)

For example:
este antibiótico   this antibiotic   **estos antibióticos**   these antibiotics
esta medicina   this medicine   **estas medicinas**   these medicines

Speaking Exercises

1. Listen to the dialog **"Sigo con dolores en los pies"** again (CD track 32). You will see how much you will understand this time! Then go to page 87 and read the dialog aloud, changing the information provided by the patient.

2. Practice expressing pain in the following parts of the body. Remember to use *me duele...* for singular and *me duelen...* for plural.

la cabeza (head)	**las mamas, los senos** (breasts)
la espalda (back)	**las articulaciones de la cadera** (hip joints)
la cintura (waist)	**las piernas** (legs)
las plantas de los pies (soles of the feet)	**la columna vertebral** (spinal column)
el pecho (chest)	**las manos** (hands)
el cuello (neck)	**los tobillos** (ankles)
el abdomen (abdomen)	**los hombros** (shoulders)

3. Practice! Say the following parts of the body in Spanish: neck, breasts, back, soles of feet, chest, hands, shoulders, abdomen, ankles, joints.

4. When do you have more pain? Using the prompts below, make up a complete sentence that describes the part of the body, the time of day, and the activity.

For example:
<u>Me duele</u> la cabeza a la mañana <u>cuando</u> me levanto.
<u>Me duelen</u> los brazos <u>cuando</u> hago ejercicio.

¿Qué le duele?		**¿Cuándo tiene más dolor?**
What hurts (you)?		When do you have more pain?
los oídos		cuando me levanto
la cabeza		cuando me siento
las piernas	a la madrugada	cuando me acuesto
los brazos	a la mañana	cuando me ducho
la espalda	al mediodía	cuando camino
el cuello	a la tarde	cuando toso
los hombros	a la noche	cuando hago ejercicio
las plantas de los pies		cuando leo en la cama
las manos		cuando trabajo
la cintura		cuando trabajo en la computadora

5. Ask your patient whether he or she took the medicine you gave or prescribed the last time.

> For example:
> <u>Did you take</u> the medicine <u>I gave you?</u>   **<u>¿Tomó</u> la medicina <u>que le di?</u>**
> <u>Did you take</u> the syrup <u>I prescribed you?</u>   **<u>¿Tomó</u> el jarabe <u>que le prescribí?</u>**

Continue asking questions with the following prompts:

the anti-inflammatory I gave you   the antacid I gave you

the medicine I prescribed you   the contraceptive I prescribed you

the antibiotic I prescribed you   the pills I prescribed you

6. Tell your patient to take the following medicines, as required.

> For example:
> this pill every six hours
> **Tome esta píldora cada seis horas.**

Remember to use the corresponding demonstrative adjective: *este, esta, estos, estas.*

Continue:

this medicine before meals   this cough syrup every eight hours

these tablets between meals   this antibiotic every twelve hours

this anti-inflammatory after meals   this contraceptive every day

Written Exercises

1. Translate (this: *este, esta*; these: *estos, estas*).

this anti-inflammatory   (a)_____

these medicines   (b)_____

this nasal decongestant   (c)_____

this syrup   (d)_____

these contraceptive pills   (e)_____

this antibiotic   (f)_____

this tablet   (g)_____

2. Translate.

Take these pills every eight hours.   (a)_____

Take this anti-inflammatory with meals.   (b)_____

Take this medicine before meals.   (c)_____

Take this cough syrup in the morning.   (d)_____

Take these contraceptive pills every day. (e)_____

Take these capsules after meals.   (f)_____

Take these antacids before meals.   (g)_____

3. How would your patient express pain in the following parts of the body?

Me duele el, la...   **Me duelen los, las...**

ojos (eyes)   (a)_____

cabeza (head)   (b)_____

caderas (hips)   (c)_____

estómago (stomach)   (d)_____

oídos (ears, internal)   (e)_____

axilas (armpits)   (f)_____

dedos (fingers)   (g)_____

espalda (back)   (h)_____

rodillas (knees)   (i)_____

pies (feet)   (j)_____

intestinos (bowels)   (k)_____

4. Complete the following sentences. Use the verbs in parentheses in the past tense. If you need help, go back to the grammar section of this chapter or check the past tense guide in Appendix 2, Verb References.

El doctor le (a)_____(prescribir) un antihistamínico al paciente López.

La doctora le (b)_____ (indicar) un plan de dieta a la Sra. Fernández.

Sra. Gómez, su médico general ya me (c)_____(informar) al respecto.

El examen de embarazo de la Sra. María Vélez (d)_____(dar) positivo.

El doctor me (e)_____(prescribir) antibióticos.

Enfermera, ¿la paciente Suárez (f)_____(tomar) la medicación?

Sra., ¿le (g)_____ (dar) el jarabe a su hijo?

El cirujano me (h)_____ (informar) acerca de los riesgos de la anestesia.

La nutricionista me (i)_____(indicar) una nueva dieta para mi tratamiento.

Role-Playing Exercise

Segunda visita al médico *Second Visit to the Doctor*

In the following situation <u>you are a podiatrist</u>. Your patient Patricio Ramírez visits you for the second time, as his pain in the left ankle persists. You ask him about his pain and whether he took the medicines you prescribed the last time. You order another X-ray, and then you change either the dose of the same medicine or the medicine itself. Listen to the following dialog when he makes the appointment with your secretary, and fill in the blanks below. You can check your comprehension of Dialog 1 in the Answer Key, in Appendix 3, at the end of the book. Then see your patient in your office.

Listen to the dialog and fill in the blanks.

Dialog 1: Scheduling the Appointment

Secretaria: **Buenas tardes, oficina de podiatría del Dr. Medina.**

Paciente: **Buenas tardes, soy Patricio Ramírez. Yo vi al doctor hace quince días, pero**

(a)_____ (b)_____ **dolores y nece-**

sito una nueva cita.

Secretaria: **Bien, ¿cuándo quiere venir?**

Paciente: **Esta semana, el (c)_____ o el**

(d)_____.

Secretaria: **Bien, hay un turno disponible el jueves a las tres de la tarde. ¿Cuál es el motivo entonces, dolor en la pierna?**

Paciente: **Dolor en mi (e) _____ y talón**

(f)_____.

Secretaria: **Bien. Hasta el jueves.**

Paciente: (g)_____. (h)_____ **el jueves.**

Now, interact with your patient.

Dialog 2: In Your Office

You: (Greet him, then ask him how he is.)
Paciente: **Así, así, doctor. Sigo con muchos dolores en el tobillo y en el talón.**
You: (Ask him when he has more pain.)
Paciente: **Por la madrugada, cuando me levanto, o cuando hago un poco de ejercicio.**
You: (Ask him if he has pain during the day.)
Paciente: **A veces, cuando camino mucho también, y además no puedo jugar al tenis.**
You: (Ask if he took the anti-inflammatory you gave him.)
Paciente: **Sí, doctor. Tomé el antiinflamatorio.**
You: (Say you are going to take another X-ray.)

Después de la radiografía
Paciente: **¿Todo bien, doctor?**
You: (Either change the dose of the medicine or give him any other relevant indications.)
Paciente: **Muy bien, doctor.**
You: (Tell him to make another appointment in 15 days.)

Chapter 10

Alimentos y nutrición

Food and Nutrition

In this chapter you will acquire all the vocabulary necessary to give a dietary plan to your patients according to their diagnoses. You will learn how to give them indications, advice, and recommendations regarding their nutritional and daily habits. You will also learn to describe and exchange information about everyday activities, speak about likes and dislikes, and consider cultural aspects related to food traditions.

Dialog: ¡Doctora, necesito y quiero bajar de peso!

Doctor, I Need and Want to Lose Weight!

 El paciente Mario Jiménez consulta a una nutricionista, por indicación de su médico general.

Patient Mario Jiménez consults a nutritionist on the advice of his general physician.

Paciente:	**Doctora, necesito y quiero bajar de peso. Tengo sobrepeso, hipertensión y colesterol elevado.**
Doctora:	**Ya veo los análisis que me envió su médico. Bien, vamos a programar un plan de tratamiento.**
Paciente:	**¿Qué debo hacer?**
Doctora:	**Ud. debe evitar las grasas y los hidratos de carbono, y debe comer comidas livianas. Cuénteme. ¿Cómo son sus actividades cotidianas? ¿Cómo es su día típico? ¿Qué come habitualmente?**
Paciente:	**Me levanto a las siete de la mañana. Me ducho y desayuno sólo café. Voy a la oficina a las ocho. Al mediodía almuerzo un sándwich o alguna comida rápida. A la tarde tengo hambre y como galletas o tostadas con café o gaseosas. Y cuando regreso a mi casa me siento cansado y sigo con mucha hambre.**
Doctora:	**¿Hace ejercicio durante el día?**
Paciente:	**No, no hago ejercicio. No tengo tiempo.**
Doctora:	**¿Y a qué hora cena?**
Paciente:	**Ceno muy tarde, a las ocho y media o nueve de la noche.**

Doctora:	**¿Come mucho en la cena?**
Paciente:	**Sí, como dos o tres porciones.**
Doctora:	**¿Y a qué hora se acuesta?**
Paciente:	**Me acuesto alrededor de las diez...**
	Doctora, ¿me va a dar alguna medicación para controlar el apetito? Es muy difícil para mí hacer dieta.
Doctora:	**No es necesario. Le recomiendo hacer cuatro comidas principales por día, en cantidades proporcionadas. Esto es muy importante para no sentir hambre. Aquí tiene un plan de dieta.**
Paciente:	**¿Cada cuánto me va a controlar?**
Doctora:	**Vamos a hacer el próximo control en quince días. Le recomiendo caminar después de almorzar y de cenar. Es muy importante para sentirse mejor y perder peso más fácilmente. Nos vemos en quince días.**

Dialog Comprehension

Test your comprehension of the dialog by checking the correct options.

¿Quién le indicó al paciente hacer una cita con un médico nutricionista?

su médico general ☐
un médico general ☐
su alergista ☐

Mr. Mario Jiménez is consulting with a:

male nutritionist ☐
female nutritionist ☐
can't determine from context ☐

The patient's diagnosis is:

overweight ☐
hypertension ☐
allergy to certain foods ☐
constipation ☐
high cholesterol ☐

The expression *tengo hambre* means:

I am thirsty. ☐
I am hungry. ☐
I am tired. ☐

When the patient says *Como dos o tres porciones,* he is saying:

I eat at two or three o'clock. ☐
I eat two or three types of food. ☐
I eat two or three servings. ☐

Does the doctor give the patient any medication to help control his appetite?

yes ☐

no ☐

I don't know. ☐

When will the patient be checked again?

in two weeks ☐

in a month ☐

in two months ☐

 Vocabulary Practice

In this section you will find words and phrases necessary to ask your patient about daily routine activities and to give recommendations. You will also learn a lot of vocabulary regarding foods.

Comidas y verbos afines *Meals and Related Verbs*

desayuno	breakfast	**desayunar**	to have breakfast
almuerzo	lunch	**almorzar**	to have lunch
merienda	afternoon snack	**merendar**	to have an afternoon snack
cena	dinner	**cenar**	to have dinner

Expresando necesidad y deseos *Expressing Needs and Wishes*

necesito	I need
quiero	I want

For example:

Necesito y quiero bajar de peso.

I need and want to lose weight.

Necesito hacer una dieta.

I need to go on a diet.

Quiero hacer dieta pero necesito recomendaciones específicas.

I want to go on a diet but I need specific recommendations.

Actividades cotidianas *Daily Activities*

¿Cómo es su día típico?	What is your typical day like?
Me levanto a las siete de la mañana.	I get up at 7:00 A.M.
Me ducho a las siete y quince.	I shower at 7:15.
Desayuno a las siete y cincuenta.	I have breakfast at 7:50.
Llevo a los niños a la escuela a las ocho.	I take the kids to school at 8:00.
Voy a trabajar a las ocho y quince.	I go to work at 8:15.
Voy a la oficina muy temprano.	I go to the office very early.
Almuerzo a las doce del mediodía.	I have lunch at 12:00 noon.

Recojo a los niños de la escuela a las tres.   I pick up the kids from school at 3:00.
Regreso a mi casa a las siete de la noche.   I get back home at 7:00 P.M.
Ceno muy tarde, a las nueve de la noche.   I have dinner very late, at 9:00 P.M.
Me acuesto alrededor de las diez.   I go to bed at around 10:00.
Me duermo a eso de las once.   I go to sleep at about 11:00.
Voy al gimnasio todas las mañanas.   I go to the gym every morning.
Salgo todos los fines de semana.   I go out every weekend.
Hago/No hago ejercicio.   I do/I don't exercise.
Juego al tenis y al fútbol.   I play tennis and football.
Voy a la playa todos los días que puedo.   I go to the beach all the days I can.

Expresando obligación *Expressing Obligation*

Usted debería...   You should...
Usted debe...   You must...
Usted tiene que...   You have to...
    seguir una dieta especial   follow a special diet
    evitar las grasas   avoid fats
    evitar los hidratos de carbono   avoid carbohydrates
    comer comidas livianas   eat light foods, meals
    controlar su apetito   control your appetite

Haciendo recomendaciones *Making Recommendations*

Le recomiendo...   I recommend that you...
    hacer cuatro comidas diarias   eat four daily meals
    caminar después de las comidas   walk after meals
    hacer ejercicio   exercise
    consultar con un especialista   consult with a specialist

Valores nutricionales *Nutrition Facts*

alimentos bajos en...   foods low in...
alimentos con bajo contenido de...   foods with a low content of...
alimentos altos en...   foods high in...
alimentos con alto contenido de...   foods with a high content of...
    azúcar   sugar
    calcio   calcium
    carbohidratos, hidratos de carbono   carbohydrates
    colesterol   cholesterol
    grasas   fat
    hierro   iron
    proteínas   protein
    potasio   potassium
    sodio   sodium

Alimentos *Foods*

CARNES Y AVES *Meats and Poultry*

tocino	bacon
(carne de) vaca	beef
pollo	chicken
jamón	ham
salchicha	sausage (hot dog)
(carne de) cordero	lamb
hígado	liver
(carne de) cerdo	pork
chorizo	sausage
bistec	steak
pavo	turkey

PESCADOS Y MARISCOS *Fish and Seafood*

almeja	clam
abadejo	cod
cangrejo	crab
langosta	lobster
salmón	salmon
camarones	shrimp
tilapia	tilapia
pez espada	swordfish
atún	tuna

VEGETALES, VERDURAS *Vegetables*

albahaca	basil
zanahoria	carrot
apio	celery
pepino	cucumber
berenjena	eggplant
ajo	garlic
lechuga	lettuce
cebolla	onion
perejil	parsley
papa	potato
zapallo, calabaza	pumpkin
remolacha	red beet
soja	soy
espinaca	spinach
calabaza	squash
tomate	tomato

LEGUMBRES SECAS Y NUECES *Dry Legumes and Nuts*

almendras	almonds
frijoles, porotos, habichuelas	beans
castañas	chestnuts
garbanzos	chick peas
avellanas	hazelnuts
lentejas	lentils
maníes, cacahuetes	peanuts
arvejas	peas
nueces	walnuts

FRUTAS *Fruits*

manzana	apple
damasco	apricot
aguacate	avocado
banana, guineo	banana
arándano azul	blueberry
cerezas	cherries
coco	coconut
arándano rojo	cranberry
dátiles	dates
higo	fig
pomelo	grapefruit
uvas	grapes
kiwi	kiwi
mango	mango
melón	melon
naranja	orange
durazno	peach
piña, ananá	pineapple
ciruela	plum
granada	pomegranate
ciruelas secas	prunes
pasas de uva	raisins
frambuesa	raspberry
fresa, frutilla	strawberry
sandía	watermelon

PRODUCTOS LÁCTEOS *Dairy Products*

manteca, mantequilla	butter
queso	cheese
queso crema	cream cheese
leche	milk
sin lactosa	lactose-free
descremada	skim
entera	whole
yogur	yogurt

HUEVOS *Eggs*

sustituto de huevo	egg substitute
clara	egg white
huevo frito	fried egg
huevo duro	hard-boiled egg
huevo al agua, poché	poached egg
huevos revueltos	scrambled eggs
yema	yolk

CEREALES *Cereals*

cebada	barley	
salvado	bran	
malta	malt	
avena	oat	
arroz	rice	
blanco		white
integral		brown
centeno	rye	
trigo	wheat	

HARINAS Y PASTAS *Breads and Pastas*

galletas, bizcochos	cookies	
pan	bread	
blanco		white
integral		whole grain
fideos	noodles	
pastas	pasta	
pizza	pizza	
empanadas	turnovers	

POSTRES *Desserts*

manzanas asadas	baked apples
tortas	cakes
flan	caramel custard
queso y dulce	cheese and jam
ensalada de frutas	fruit salad
helado	ice cream
gelatina	gelatin
duraznos en almíbar	peaches in syrup
tartas	pies

BEBIDAS *Drinks*

cerveza	beer
leche chocolatada	chocolate milk
café	coffee
jugos, licuados de frutas	fruit juices, shakes
agua mineral	mineral water
gaseosas, sodas	sodas
agua con gas, soda	sparkling water
mate, mate cocido	mate tea
té	tea

CONDIMENTOS, ADEREZOS Y VARIOS
Seasonings, Dressings, and Others

vinagre balsámico	balsamic vinegar	
mermelada	marmalade	
aceite	oil	
de maíz		corn
de girasol		sunflower
de oliva		olive
pimienta	pepper	
roja, ají molido		red pepper
negra		black pepper
sal	salt	
salsa	sauce	
azúcar	sugar	
edulcorante	sugar substitute, sweetener	
dulces	sweets	
vinagre	vinegar	

MODOS DE COCCIÓN *Cooking Methods*

al horno	baked, roasted
carne <u>al horno</u>	<u>baked</u> meat
hervido, -a	boiled
pollo <u>hervido</u>	<u>boiled</u> chicken
rápido, -a	fast
comida rápida	fast food
frito, -a	fried
papas <u>fritas</u>	<u>fried</u> potatoes
a la parrilla	grilled
pescado <u>a la parrilla</u>	<u>grilled</u> fish
semi-cocido, a punto	medium
jugoso, -a	rare
bien cocido	well-done
bistec <u>bien cocido</u>	<u>well-done</u> steak
crudo, -a	raw
carne <u>cruda</u>	<u>raw</u> meat
al vapor	steamed
verduras <u>al vapor</u>	<u>steamed</u> vegetables

Desórdenes o trastornos alimenticios que pueden requerir una dieta especial
Disorders That May Require a Special Diet

celiaquía	celiac disease
colitis	colitis
estreñimiento	constipation
diabetes	diabetes
glucosa elevada	elevated glucose
gastritis	gastritis
gastroenterocolitis	gastroenterocolitis
colesterol elevado	high cholesterol
sobrepeso	overweight
sobrepeso en el embarazo	overweight during pregnancy

Grammar in Use

Expressing Wishes

Verb *querer* (to want) + infinitive

quiero (first person singular) I want

For example:
Quiero comenzar a hacer deportes.	I want to start playing sports.
Quiero hablar con usted.	I want to speak to you.

Verbs, Simple Present Tense

desayunar	to have breakfast
desayuno (first person singular)	I have breakfast
desayuna (third person singular)	you (formal) have breakfast; he, she has breakfast

For example:
¿A qué hora desayuna?	At what time do you have breakfast?
Desayuno a las siete y cincuenta.	I have breakfast at 7:50.

llevar	to take (to)
llevo (first person singular)	I take
lleva (third person singular)	you (formal) take; he, she takes

For example:
Llevo a los niños a la escuela a las ocho.	I take the kids to school at 8:00.
Mi esposa lleva a los niños a la escuela.	My wife takes the kids to school.

ir	to go
voy (first person singular)	I go
va (third person singular)	you (formal) go; he, she goes

For example:
Voy al gimnasio los lunes y jueves.	I go to the gym on Mondays and Thursdays.
Mi esposo va a la oficina muy temprano.	My husband goes to the office very early.

almorzar	to have lunch
almuerz<u>o</u> (first person singular)	I have lunch
almuerz<u>a</u> (third person singular)	you (formal) have lunch; he, she has lunch

    For example:

¿Dónde <u>almuerza</u> habitualmente?	Where do <u>you have lunch</u> usually?
<u>Almuerzo</u> a las doce del mediodía.	<u>I have lunch</u> at twelve noon.

recoger (de)	pick up (from)
recoj<u>o</u> (first person singular)	I pick up
recog<u>e</u> (third person singular)	you (formal) pick up; he, she picks up

    For example:

<u>Recojo</u> a los niños <u>de</u> la escuela a las tres.	<u>I pick up</u> the kids <u>from</u> school at three.
El autobús <u>recoge</u> a los niños a las ocho.	The bus <u>picks up</u> the kids at eight.

regresar	to get back, return
regres<u>o</u> (first person singular)	I get back
regres<u>a</u> (third person singular)	you (formal) return; he, she returns

    For example:

¿<u>Regresa</u> muy tarde a su casa?	<u>Do you get back</u> home late?
<u>Regreso</u> a mi casa a las siete de la noche.	<u>I return</u> home at seven in the evening.

cenar	to have dinner
cen<u>o</u> (first person singular)	I have dinner
cen<u>a</u> (third person singular)	you (formal) have dinner; he, she has dinner

    For example:

¿A qué hora <u>cena</u>?	At what time <u>do you have dinner</u>?
<u>Ceno</u> muy tarde, a las nueve de la noche.	<u>I have dinner</u> very late, at 9:00 P.M.

Please Refer to Appendix 2, Verb Reference section, on page 135, for more information.

Reflexive Verbs

Notice that some of the verbs we have used to describe daily activities are reflexive. They are used with their corresponding reflexive pronouns. Reflexive verbs in Spanish consist of the main verb plus the reflexive pronoun *se.*

    For example:

levantar(se)	to get (oneself) up
duchar(se)	to shower (oneself)
acostar(se)	to go to bed, to lie (oneself) down

The reflexive pronoun refers to the receiver of the action of the verb, thus we have:

yo (I)	**me**	**nosotros** (we)	**nos**
tú (informal you)	**te**	**ustedes** (you)	**se**
usted, él, ella (formal you, he, she)	**se**	**ellos** (they)	**se**

Reflexive verbs are conjugated in the same way as non-reflexive verbs, but they are preceded by the corresponding reflexive pronoun. Observe the difference between the use of the same verb when referring to oneself (reflexive), or when referring to someone else (non-reflexive).

despertar	to wake up

For example:
Yo <u>me despierto</u> a las siete de la mañana todos los días.
<u>I wake (myself) up</u> at seven o'clock every morning.
Yo <u>despierto a mis hijos</u> a las siete y media.
<u>I wake my children up</u> at seven thirty.

Let's see some examples with the reflexive verbs from the dialog:

levantar(se)	to get (oneself) up
me levant<u>o</u> (first person singular)	I get up
se levant<u>a</u> (third person singular)	you (formal) get up; he, she gets up

For example:
¿A qué hora <u>se levanta</u> usted?   At what time <u>do you get up</u>?
<u>Me levanto</u> a las siete de la mañana.   <u>I get up</u> at 7:00 A.M.

duchar(se)	to shower (oneself)

For example:
Mi hijo <u>se ducha</u> por la noche y mi hija <u>se ducha</u> por la mañana.
My son <u>showers</u> in the evening, and my daughter <u>showers</u> in the morning.
Yo <u>me ducho</u> dos veces por día, a la mañana y a la noche.
I <u>shower</u> twice a day, in the morning and at night.

Pay attention to the use of reflexive pronouns in the "you/I" relationship between doctor and patient.

levantar(se)	to get up

For example:
¿<u>Se levanta</u> a orinar durante la noche?   <u>Do you get up</u> to urinate at night?
Sí, doctor, <u>me levanto</u> varias veces.   Yes, doctor, <u>I get up</u> many times.
¿Cuántas veces <u>se levanta</u>?   How many times <u>do you get up</u>?
<u>Me levanto</u> tres o cuatro veces.   <u>I get up</u> three or four times.

acostar(se)	to go to bed, to lie down

For example:
¿<u>Se acuesta</u> muy tarde?   <u>Do you go to bed</u> very late?
<u>Me acuesto</u> a las diez de la noche.   <u>I go to bed</u> at 10:00 P.M.

bañar(se)	to bathe

For example:
¿<u>Se baña</u> solo?   <u>Do you bathe</u> alone?
Sí, doctor, <u>me baño</u> solo.   Yes, doctor, <u>I bathe</u> alone.

Asking Questions

As you may have noticed, to ask questions regarding habits or everyday life we just need the question word, when relevant, followed by the corresponding conjugated verb in the present tense, plus the time reference, if any.

For example:

¿Qué come habitualmente?	What do you usually eat?
¿A qué hora almuerza?	What time do you have lunch?
¿Practica deportes los fines de semana?	Do you play sports on the weekends?
¿Qué hace los domingos?	What do you do on Sundays?

Expressing Obligation

deber **+** infinitive verb	must, should + infinitive verb
tener que **+** infinitive verb	have to + infinitive verb

For example:

Usted debe...	You must...
Usted debería...	You should...
Usted tiene que...	You have to...
comenzar una dieta	start a diet
hacer ejercicio	exercise
dejar de fumar	quit smoking
fumar menos	smoke less
comer comidas sanas	eat healthy food
organizar su trabajo	organize your work
dormir más	sleep more

Expressing Recommendations

Verb *recomendar* **+** infinitive verb

Le recomiendo...	I recommend that you...
hacer cuatro comidas diarias	eat four daily meals
caminar después de las comidas	walk after meals
hacer ejercicio	exercise
consultar con un especialista	consult with a specialist

Expressing Objectives, Purpose

¿Para qué?	What for?
para...	to...

Infinitival phrases introduced by **to + infinitive verb,** used to indicate purpose in English, are equivalent to the construction **preposition** *para* **+ infinitive verb** in Spanish.

For example:

<u>**para**</u> **no sentir hambre**	<u>to</u> not be hungry (feel hunger)
<u>**para**</u> **sentirse mejor**	<u>to</u> feel better
<u>**para**</u> **perder peso más facilmente**	<u>to</u> lose weight more easily
<u>**para**</u> **bajar el nivel de colesterol**	<u>to</u> lower the cholesterol level
<u>**para**</u> **obtener un bienestar general**	<u>to</u> achieve general wellness

A Note on Feminine Nouns Starting with Stressed Vowel <u>*a*</u>: noun-adjective agreement
The noun *hambre* is of feminine nature. Nevertheless, it will take the article *el,* as many other feminine words that start with stressed vowel *a;* for example, the so frequently used word *agua* (water). Because they are feminine, all the adjectives modifying these words will be feminine. We will then say, for example: *"Tengo much<u>a</u> hambre"* (I am very hungry), or *"El agu<u>a</u> está fría"* (The water is cold). You can revisit Chapter 2 (page 12) for more information on agreement of nouns and adjectives.

Speaking Exercises

1. Go to page 98 and read aloud the dialog **"¡Doctora, necesito y quiero bajar de peso!"** again. You will see how much easier and more familiar it is to you now.

2. The following patients have been diagnosed with different disorders. Give them indications regarding a dietary plan, according to each problem. See the guide below for help. Review the structures and vocabulary if necessary!

> Patient 1: **Doctor, ¿Qué me recomienda para mi problema de colesterol?**
> Patient 2: **Doctor, me han diagnosticado gastroenterocolitis. ¿Qué tengo que comer y tomar?**
> Patient 3: **Doctora, tengo 50 libras de sobrepeso, pero me es muy difícil hacer dieta.**
> Patient 4: **Doctor, no puedo mover los intestinos. ¿Qué me recomienda para el estreñimiento?**
> Patient 5: **Doctora, mis análisis de sangre evidencian glucosa elevada.**

VOCABULARY

Usted debe, Usted debería, Usted tiene que...	You must, You should, you have to...
evitar los hidratos de carbono	avoid carbohydrates
reducir las calorías diarias	reduce daily calories
comer más vegetales y frutas	eat more vegetables and fruits
beber mucha agua	drink plenty of water
comer comidas livianas	eat light meals
evitar las comidas pesadas	avoid heavy meals
Usted no debe...	You mustn't...
beber alcohol	drink alcohol
comer comidas picantes	eat spicy foods
comer comidas altas en grasas	eat high-fat foods
fumar	smoke
Le recomiendo...	I recommend that you...
hacer ejercicio	exercise
caminar después de comer	walk after eating
hacer cuatro comidas por día	eat four meals a day
comer comidas livianas	eat light foods
comer alimentos con fibra	eat foods with fiber
practicar un deporte	play a sport
hacer gimnasia	go to the gym
nadar	swim
andar en bicicleta	ride a bike

3. You are a nutritionist trying to learn about your patient's everyday activities in order to design a suitable plan for him or her. Translate the following questions.

What is your typical day like?   Do you exercise?
What do you have for breakfast?   Do you play sports?
What time do you have lunch?   Do you smoke?
Describe what you usually eat in the afternoon.   Do you drink too much coffee?
At what time do you have dinner?   Do you drink water during the day?

4. Ask a patient if he or she likes a certain food. Look at the examples first.

gustar   to like
¿Le gusta...?   Do you like (food in singular)?

    For example:
    <u>¿Le gusta</u> la espinaca?   Do you like spinach?

Ask your patient if he or she likes the following items:

la remolacha (beet)   **el pescado** (fish)
el pollo hervido (boiled chicken)   **el arroz** (rice)
la carne asada (baked meat)   **el hígado** (liver)

Now observe the same question when referring to a plural noun.

¿Le gusta<u>n</u>...?   Do you like (food in plural)?

    For example:
    <u>¿Le gustan</u> las lentejas?   Do you like lentils?

Ask your patient if he or she likes the following items:

los frijoles (beans)   **las verduras al vapor** (steamed vegetables)
los vegetales (vegetables)   **las pastas** (pasta)
las frutas (fruits)   **las nueces** (nuts)

5. Nutritionist Charlotte López has prepared this basic survey to learn about her patients' likes and dislikes. Pretend you are one of her patients and fill out the survey according to your likes and dislikes.

¿Es alérgico a algún alimento?	**sí**	**no**
Si es alérgico, ¿a qué alimentos?	———————————	
¿Le gustan las carnes rojas?	**sí**	**no**
las aves?	**sí**	**no**
los pescados?	**sí**	**no**
las pastas?	**sí**	**no**
las frutas?	**sí**	**no**
las verduras?	**sí**	**no**
¿Qué le gusta para beber?		
agua	**sí**	**no**
agua con gas	**sí**	**no**
jugos de frutas	**sí**	**no**
licuados de frutas	**sí**	**no**
¿Qué le gusta de postre?		
frutas frescas	**sí**	**no**
manzana asada	**sí**	**no**
helado	**sí**	**no**
quesos con frutas	**sí**	**no**
gelatina	**sí**	**no**
duraznos en almíbar	**sí**	**no**

6. Let's practice the vocabulary in a different way now! At home, go to the kitchen and practice by opening the fridge, the freezer, and the kitchen cabinets and saying the names of the objects you see aloud. It will be even better if you actually touch or grasp the object while you do this exercise. If you come across an item you don't know or that is not in the vocabulary section, refer to a dictionary.

Written Exercises

1. Can you translate these sentences?

You should avoid fatty foods.

(a)_____

You must not smoke.

(b)_____

You should avoid fried foods.

(c)_____

You have to follow a diet.

(d)_____

You must avoid alcohol.

(e)_____

2. Put the following sentences in the correct order to form a complete dialog, and translate the title. Write a number in each blank to indicate the correct order of the sentences. The first and the last doctor's comments are already in the right place.

In the Nutritionist's Consulting Room

(a)_____

_____ Doctora: **Buenos días, señora García.**

_____ Paciente: **Cenamos a las nueve de la noche, y a esa hora tenemos mucha hambre.**

_____ Doctora: **¿Desayuna antes de salir de su casa?**

_____ Paciente: **Me levanto a las ocho de la mañana, llevo a mis niños a la escuela, y voy a trabajar a mi oficina.**

_____ Doctora: **¿A qué hora cena?**

_____ Paciente: **Vengo referida por mi médico general, por sobrepeso. No puedo bajar de peso, y mis dietas son un continuo fracaso.**

_____ Paciente: **Buenos días, doctora.**

_____ Doctora: **¿Y a qué hora almuerza? ¿Dónde almuerza?**

_____ Paciente: **A veces desayuno cereales con leche, otras veces café con "bagels" y queso crema, y a veces tostadas con un poco de mantequilla y un huevo frito.**

_____ Doctora: **Cuénteme, ¿cuál es el motivo de su visita?**

_____ Paciente: **Al mediodía almuerzo en mi oficina, un sándwich con papitas fritas, o ensaladas, o una comida rápida.**

_____ Doctora: **Bien. Cuénteme. ¿Cómo es su día típico?¿A qué hora se levanta?**

_____ Paciente: **No tengo tiempo para hacer ejercicio. Cuando regreso a mi casa, tengo que atender a mis hijos, ayudarlos con sus tareas de la escuela, bañarlos, hacer la cena, y cuando mi marido regresa cenamos.**

_____ Doctora: **¿Hace ejercicio?**

_____ Doctora: **Bien... vamos a programar un plan de alimentación y vamos a revisar los hábitos alimenticios desde el desayuno hasta la cena.**

Role-Playing Exercise

Comidas y nutrición *Food and Nutrition*

In the following situation <u>you are a nutritionist</u> interviewing a patient who has been diagnosed with hypertension, overweight, and high cholesterol. Give him general directions for a four-meal-a-day basic diet. Make sure you can handle the vocabulary and structures before doing the exercise.

P: **Doctor, ¿qué me recomienda en el desayuno?**
You: (Let him know that you recommend fruit juice, fruits, and cereals.)
P: **Bien. ¿Puedo comer huevos?**
You: (Let him know you recommend eating egg whites, four or five times a week only.)
P: **Bien. ¿Y en el almuerzo?**
You: (Let him know you recommend salads with lemon juice and no salt, vegetables, brown rice, low-fat meats, or chicken breast.)
P: **¿Y qué me recomienda a la tarde, como merienda?**
You: (low-fat yogurts, cereals, or fruit juices, and at night the same as for lunch)
P: **Bien, doctor. Trataré de hacer la dieta como usted me indica.**

Cultural Information

Food and culture are so closely related that it would take a long time to learn about each people's food traditions with accuracy. Do you think you could complete the following chart by searching the Internet for these common foods found in Spanish-speaking countries? See the first example:

Typical dish	Country	Brief description
burritos	México	rolled tortilla filled with meat or beans, cheese, and vegetables
fajitas		
sancocho		
arepas		
quesadilla		
ceviche		
tortillas		
arroz con coco		
arroz con frijoles		
asopao		
ropa vieja		
asado		
chivito		
mate (drink)		
paella		

Chapters 6 to 10 Self-Check Exercise

1. Cross out the word that does not belong in each row.

   (a) espalda   brazo   estómago   cabeza   palpitaciones

   (b) obstetra   hijo   madre   suegro   abuela

   (c) nutricionista   pediatra   fruta   cardiólogo   dermatólogo

   (d) comida   cápsula   jarabe   pastilla   tableta

   (e) piernas   pies   brazos   manos   sobrepeso

   (f) nombre   camilla   domicilio   teléfono   seguro social

   (g) vesícula   abuelo   nieto   padrino   padrastro

   (h) tomate   lechuga   zanahoria   salmón   papa

   (i) náuseas   vómitos   mareos   análisis   diarrea

   (j) naranja   leche   manzana   banana   ciruela

2. Circle the correct word.

   La paciente del Dr. Pérez (a)_____ en la sala de espera.   **es**   **está**   **soy**

   Mi padre (b)_____ un poco asustado.   **está**   **trabajo**   **soy**

   ¿Para (c)_____ necesita su próxima cita?   **cómo**   **cuándo**   **dónde**

   ¿(d)_____ hace que tiene dolor en el pecho?   **cuál**   **dónde**   **cuánto**

   El paciente Gómez (e)_____ mucho dolor en las piernas.   **tiene**   **tengo**   **está**

3. What specialists will hear these questions and complaints?

   Doctor, tengo mucho sobrepeso. Necesito hacer una dieta.   (a)_____

   Doctor, mi hija de tres años tiene fiebre alta y tos.   (b)_____

   Doctor, necesito hacerme un chequeo general.   (c)_____

Doctor, por las noches cuando me acuesto siento taquicardia
y falta de aire. Estoy un poco asustado.   (d)_____

Mi médico general me ha referido por una infección urinaria.   (e)_____

4. Match the corresponding sentences.

(a) ¿A qué hora es su cita con el doctor?   1. ¿Dónde siente los dolores exactamente?

(b) ¿Dónde almuerza habitualmente?   2. ¡Mucho gusto, señor Juan!

(c) Doctor, tengo dolores musculares.   3. Tome la medicina cada ocho horas.

(d) ¿Cuándo tiene más dolor?   4. En algún restaurante cerca de mi oficina.

(e) ¿Cómo es el paciente Peralta?   5. En el primer piso, a la izquierda.

(f) Doctor, él es Juan, mi marido.   6. Mi cita es a las nueve de la mañana.

(g) ¿Dónde está la sala de radiología?   7. A la mañana, cuando me levanto.

(h) ¿Cuándo tengo que tomar la medicina?   8. Está mejor, ahora está más tranquila.

(i) ¿Cómo está la paciente Domínguez?   9. Es un señor mayor. Es delgado y calvo.

5. Associate each diagnosis with the corresponding recommendations.

(a) hipertensión arterial   1. Para bajar de peso deberá seguir una dieta estricta.

(b) sobrepeso/obesidad   2. No debe comer comidas con sal.

(c) glucosa elevada   3. Voy a darle un laxante y le recomiendo comer ciruelas secas.

(d) estreñimiento   4. Usted no debe consumir alimentos con azúcar.

(e) colesterol elevado   5. Usted debe evitar las grasas y las comidas fritas y picantes.

Chapter 11

La historia médica

The Medical History

In this chapter you will learn to conduct a medical interview, going through the patient's medical and family history. You will be able to design a medical history interview that is tailored to your own professional needs.

Dialog: Consultando al gastroenterólogo

Consulting the Gastroenterologist

 La Sra. María Lares va al consultorio del Dr. Sánchez, especialista en gastroenterología.
Mrs. María Lares goes to the office of Dr. Sánchez, a specialist in gastroenterology.

María:	**Buenos días. Soy la Sra. Lares.**
Recepcionista:	**Sí, buenos días, Sra. Lares. Aquí tengo sus datos. Usted ha sido referida por su médico general, ¿verdad?**
María:	**Así es.**
Recepcionista:	**Por favor, complete estos formularios con sus datos personales y sus antecedentes médicos. El Dr. Sánchez ya la atiende.**
Con el Dr. Sánchez	
María:	**Buenos Días, Dr. Sánchez.**
Dr. Sánchez:	**Buenos Días, Sra. Lares. ¿Cómo está? Aquí tengo los informes que me ha enviado su médico general.**
María:	**Sí, doctor. Sigo con muchas molestias en el estómago, y estoy un poco preocupada.**
Dr. Sánchez:	**¿Cómo son esas molestias?**
María:	**Tengo dolores y ardor, especialmente después de comer. He seguido una dieta, pero los dolores no ceden.**
Dr. Sánchez:	**¿Puede describir los síntomas con más exactitud?**
María:	**Siento dolor agudo aquí en el estómago, acidez, ardor, y a veces siento como puntadas.**
Dr. Sánchez:	**¿Tiene náuseas y vómitos?**
María:	**Tengo náuseas frecuentemente y regurgitaciones.**

Dr. Sánchez:	**¿Tiene vómitos?**
María:	**No.**
Dr. Sánchez:	**Bien. Vamos a hacer un análisis de sangre y de orina. Además voy a indicarle una radiografía de estómago, y vamos a hacer una endoscopía.**
María:	**¿Doctor, me va a dar algún tratamiento?**
Dr. Sánchez:	**Le voy a indicar una dieta, hasta tener los resultados de los estudios. Por favor, haga una nueva cita en quince días.**

Dialog Comprehension

Test your comprehension of the dialog by checking the correct options.

La Señora María Lares está en el consultorio del:

médico clínico	☐
dermatólogo	☐
gastroenterólogo	☐

¿Qué estudios le indica el Dr. Sánchez a la paciente Lares?

análisis de sangre	☐
análisis de orina	☐
ecografía de estómago	☐
radiografía de estómago	☐
ecografía de vesícula	☐
endoscopía	☐

El Dr. Sánchez:

le indica una dieta	☐
le prescribe medicinas	☐
necesita los resultados de los estudios	☐

🄾 Vocabulary Practice

In this section you will incorporate useful questions and vocabulary necessary to learn and be very specific about your patient's pain. You will learn vocabulary and phrases necessary to conduct a medical history, reviewing the patient's medical history and family history.

Verificando las referencias con el paciente *Checking Referrals with the Patient*

Sr. López, usted ha sido referido por su médico general, ¿verdad?
Mr. López, you have been referred by your general physician, haven't you?
Sra. Pérez, usted ha sido derivada por su médico general, ¿verdad?
Mrs. Pérez, you have been referred by your general physician, haven't you?

Here is a list of questions you may ask your patient to learn more about his or her pain. By this point, you are already using some of these, but review this important group of questions.

¿Cuánto tiempo hace que tiene dolor?	How long have you had the pain?
¿Cuándo siente más dolor?	When do you feel more pain?
¿Dónde tiene el dolor?	Where do you have the pain?
¿Hacia dónde se expande?	Where does it radiate?
¿Cómo es el dolor exactamente?	What is the pain like exactly?
¿Cómo es el dolor en una escala de 1 a 10?	How is the pain on a scale from 1 to 10?
¿Le duele aquí?	Does it hurt here?
¿Qué le alivia el dolor?	What relieves the pain?
¿Qué se lo mejora?	What makes it better?
¿Qué se lo empeora?	What makes it worse?
¿Qué provocó el dolor?	What brought this pain on?
¿Es intermitente o constante?	Is it intermittent or constant?

Here is a list of words patients might use to refer to kinds of pain.

Siento...; Tengo...	I feel...; I have...
cólicos	colic
espasmos	spasms
miedo a sentir dolor	fear of feeling pain
puntadas	stitches, sharp pains
cuchilladas	stabbing pains
un dolor fuerte	a strong pain
un dolor leve	a mild pain
un dolor muy intenso	a very intense pain
un dolor punzante	a sharp pain
un dolor que no cede	a pain that does not ease
una opresión	oppression, tightness

Historia médica del paciente *Patient's Medical History*

ENFERMEDADES COMUNES DE LA INFANCIA *Common Childhood Illnesses*

¿Tuvo...?	Did you have...?
¿Ha tenido...?	Have you had...?
varicela	varicella (chicken pox)
sarampión	measles
paperas	mumps
rubeola	rubella
escarlatina	scarlet fever
viruela	smallpox

OTRAS ENFERMEDADES *Other Illnesses*

¿Tiene...?	Do you have...?
¿Ha tenido...?	Have you had...?
anemia	anemia
artritis	arthritis
asma	asthma
bronquitis	bronchitis
cáncer o tumores	cancer or tumors
diabetes	diabetes
difteria	diphtheria
nivel elevado de sedimentación	elevated sedimentation rate
problemas glandulares	gland problems
hepatitis A, B, C	hepatitis A, B, C
colesterol alto	high cholesterol
hospitalizaciones	hospitalizations
hiperglucemia (glucosa alta)	hyperglycemia (high glucose)
hipertiroidismo	hyperthyroidism
hipoglucemia (glucosa baja)	hypoglycemia (low glucose)
hipotiroidismo	hypothyroidism
infartos	infarcts, heart attacks
infecciones	infections
ictericia	jaundice
malaria	malaria
meningitis	meningitis
migrañas	migraines
problemas musculares	muscle problems
operaciones, cirugías	operations, surgeries
tosferina	pertussis, whooping cough
poliomielitis	poliomyelitis
fiebre reumática	rheumatic fever
problemas óseos	skeletal problems
amigdalitis	tonsillitis
tuberculosis	tuberculosis
tifoidea	typhoid
problemas urinarios	urinary problems
enfermedades venéreas	venereal diseases

Para mujeres solamente *For Women Only*

MENSTRUACIÓN *Menstruation*

¿A qué edad tuvo su menarca?	At what age did you have your menarche?
¿Sus menstruaciones son regulares, escasas o abundantes?	Are your periods regular, scarce, or abundant?
¿Tiene mucho dolor?	Do you have much pain?
¿Tiene irregularidades?	Do you have irregularities?
¿Cuándo fue su último período?	When was your last period?

EMBARAZOS *Pregnancies*

¿Tiene hijos?¿Cuántos?	Do you have children? How many?
¿Tuvo problemas durante su embarazo?	Did you have problems during pregnancy?
¿Tuvo inconvenientes en el parto?	Did you have problems during delivery?
¿Su parto fue vaginal?	Was your delivery vaginal?
¿Su parto fue por cesárea?	Was your delivery cesarean?
¿Sus partos fueron en término?	Were your pregnancies full-term?
¿Ha tenido abortos...?	Have you had abortions...?
naturales	natural
espontáneos	spontaneous
otros	other

Vida sexual *Sex Life*

MÉTODOS ANTICONCEPTIVOS *Contraceptive Methods*

¿Usa...?	Do you use...?
condones/preservativos	condoms
píldoras anticonceptivas	contraceptive pills
cremas	creams
diafragma	diaphragm
inyecciones	injections
espiral, DIU (dispositivo intrauterino)	IUD
el método del ritmo	rhythm method
ligadura de trompas	tubal ligation
control de temperatura vaginal	vaginal temperature method
vasectomía	vasectomy
otros	others

ENFERMEDADES VENÉREAS *Venereal Diseases*

¿Tiene...?	Do you have...?
¿Ha tenido...?	Have you had...?
clamidia	chlamydia
verrugas genitales	genital warts
gonorrea	gonorrhea
herpes	herpes
HIV, SIDA	HIV, AIDS
infecciones	infections
sífilis	syphilis
otros	others

Hábitos *Habits*

¿Fuma?	Do you smoke?
¿Cuánto?	How much?
¿Desde qué edad?	Since when?
¿Bebe alcohol?	Do you drink alcohol?
¿Cuánto?	How much?
¿Desde qué edad?	Since when?

¿Sus hábitos alimentarios son sanos?	Are your eating habits healthy?
¿Tiene dificultades con los intestinos?	Do you have trouble with your bowels?
¿Tiene problemas para orinar?	Do you have problems urinating?
¿Practica deportes?	Do you play sports?
¿Hace ejercicio?	Do you exercise?
¿Tiene problemas con el sueño?	Do you have problems sleeping?
¿Duerme ocho horas diarias?	Do you sleep eight hours a day?
¿Cuántas horas duerme?	How many hours do you sleep?
¿Tiene pareja sexual estable?	Do you have a stable sexual partner?
¿Cuál es su peso habitual?	What is your habitual weight?
¿Cuál es su peso actual?	What is your present weight?

Hospitalizaciones, operaciones, cirugías *Hospitalizations, Operations, Surgeries*

¿Ha sido hospitalizado, -a? ¿Por qué motivo?	Have you been hospitalized? Why?
¿Ha tenido operaciones?¿Cuáles?	Have you had operations? Which?
¿Ha tenido cirugías? ¿Cuáles?	Have you had surgeries? Which?
¿Le han dado anestesia general?	Have you been given general anesthesia?

Antecedentes de medicinas *Medication History*

¿Es alérgico a alguna medicina?	Are you allergic to any medicine?
¿Está tomando alguna medicina? ¿Cuál?	Are you taking any medicine? Which?
¿Ha tomado alguna medicina por mucho tiempo?	Have you taken any medicine for a long time?

Historia de la familia *Family History*

¿Hay antecedentes de ... en su familia?	Is there a history of ... in your family?
alcoholismo	alcoholism
anemia	anemia
arterioesclerosis	arteriosclerosis
artritis	arthritis
asma	asthma
cáncer	cancer
diabetes	diabetes
síndrome de Down	Down syndrome
drogas	drugs
cardiopatías	heart diseases
hepatitis	hepatitis
hipertensión arterial	hypertension
enfermedades pulmonares	lung diseases
migrañas	migraines
trastornos psiquiátricos	psychiatric disorders
tuberculosis	tuberculosis
enfermedades venéreas	venereal diseases

At this point you have all the language tools you need to design any medical history interview. You can also incorporate any vocabulary you may need from Appendix 1, Medical Specialties.

Grammar in Use

Verbs, Present Perfect Tense

haber **+ participle**   have + participle
he **+ participle:** use with the **first person** singular, *yo* (I).
ha **+ participle:** use with the **third person** singular *usted* (you), *el* (he), *ella* (she)

seguir   to follow

>   For example:
>   **He seguido una dieta.**
>   I have followed a diet.
>   **Yo he seguido una dieta esctricta.**
>   I have followed a strict diet.
>   **Usted no ha seguido las indicaciones de su médico.**
>   You have not followed your physician's instructions.

tener   to have

>   For example:
>   **¿Ha tenido problemas cardíacos?**   Have you had cardiac problems?
>   **¿Ha tenido cirugías?**   Have you had surgeries?

derivar, referir   to refer

>   For example:
>   **El doctor me ha derivado a un gastroenterólogo.**
>   The doctor has referred me to a gastroenterologist.
>   **La doctora me ha referido a un psicólogo.**
>   The doctor has referred me to a psychologist.

diagnosticar   to diagnose

>   For example:
>   **La doctora ha diagnosticado al paciente Pérez con diabetes e hipertensión.**
>   The doctor has diagnosed patient Pérez with diabetes and hypertension.

Find more information about the Present Perfect Tense in Appendix 2, Verb References, on page 137.

Passive Construction

The passive construction is formed as in English, by conjugating the verb "to be" in the same tense of the verb in the active voice sentence, plus the past participle of the main verb. Thus, we have:

ser (infinitive)   to be
sido (participle)   been

>   For example:
>   **¿Ha sido (usted) hospitalizado?**   Have you been hospitalized?
>   **Juana ha sido referida por el Dr. Vázquez.** Juana has been referred by Dr. Vásquez.
>   **Yo he sido derivado por mi médico**   I have been referred by my general
>   **general.**   physician.
>   **La paciente Yamila Márquez ha sido**   Patient Yamila Márquez has been diagnosed
>   **diagnosticada con diabetes.**   with diabetes.

Note that in passive constructions, because the participle is directly connected and referring to the subject, it is affected by gender and number in the same way adjectives are. Again, the verb always agrees in person and number with its subject. Here are more passive voice examples that illustrate this explanation.

Active voice, Simple Present:
El enfermero controla los informes médicos de los pacientes todos los días.
The nurse checks the patients' medical reports every day.

Passive voice, Simple Present:
Los informes médicos de los pacientes <u>son</u> controla<u>dos</u> todos los días.
The patient's medical reports <u>are checked</u> every day.

Active voice, Simple Past:
María compró las medicinas ayer.   María bought the medicines yesterday.

Passive voice, Simple Past:
Las medicinas <u>fueron</u> compradas ayer.   The medicines <u>were bought</u> yesterday.

Active voice, Present Perfect:
El médico ya ha visitado a todos los pacientes.   The doctor has already visited all the patients.

Passive voice, Present Perfect:
Los pacientes ya <u>han sido</u> visita<u>dos</u> por el médico.   The patients <u>have</u> already <u>been visited</u> by the doctor.

Speaking Exercises

1. Go to page 116 and read aloud the dialog **"Consultando al gastroenterólogo"** again, changing the patient's complaint and the doctor's questions and recommendations accordingly.

2. You are a receptionist. Check with each patient below that he or she has been referred by his or her general physician. You will be provided with each patient's name together with his or her physician's. Look at the examples for help.

   Sr. Giraldes, ¿usted ha sido referido por la Dra. Johnson, verdad?
   Sra. López, ¿usted ha sido referida por el Dr. Fuentes, verdad?

   Sr. Frutos / Dr. Saéz   Sr. González / Dra. Velázquez

   Sra. Benítez / Dra. Blanco   Sra. Juárez / Dr. Pintos

   Sr. Torres / Dra. Escudero

3. Think of a patient, then go to **"The Patient's Medical History"** and **"Family History"** on pages 118–121, cover the English translations, and read the Spanish sections aloud. Make sure you understand all you read, checking whenever necessary, while you also consider some possible answers your patient might give.

   Motivo de consulta del paciente:

Written Exercises

1. Translate into English:

   varicela: (a)_____

   rubeola: (b)_____

   sarampión: (c)_____

   paperas: (d)_____

   viruela: (e)_____

2. Translate into Spanish:

   Do you smoke?

   (a)_____

   What contraceptive method do you use?

   (b)_____

   What is your habitual weight?

   (c)_____

   Do you play sports?

   (d)_____

   Have you had history of diabetes in your family?

   (e)_____

3. Translate into either English or Spanish:

   ¿Ha tenido enfermedades venéreas?

   (a)_____

   Have you ever been hospitalized?

   (b)_____

   Have you had surgeries?

   (c)_____

Are you allergic to any medicine?

(d)_____

¿Le han dado (alguna vez) anestesia general?

(e)_____

Role-Playing Exercise

Historia médica *Medical History*

<u>You are the only health care professional who knows some Spanish in Dr. Scalpi's office.</u> Mara Herrera, a woman in her fifties, comes in for a general examination, because she says she "has not been to a physician for the last two years." The second reason is that she feels she needs to lose significant weight, since she also has severe back pains and shortness of breath and she says that "weight is affecting her everyday life." Act as a translator between the doctor and Mara Herrera.

Mara Herrera: **Buenos días, Dr. Scalpi. Necesito hacerme un chequeo general. Hace dos años que no voy al médico.**

You: (translate)_____

Dr. Scalpi: OK. Sit down on the examining table, please.

You: (translate)_____

Dr. Scalpi: Open your mouth.

You: (translate)_____

Dr. Scalpi: Raise your arms, please.

You: (translate)_____

Dr. Scalpi: We're going to do an electrocardiogram.

You: (translate)_____

Dr. Scalpi: And I will order a complete blood and urine test. Also, I will refer you to a gynecologist.

You: (translate)_____

Mara: **Bien, doctor. Doctor, estoy preocupada porque siento que mi peso está afectando mi vida diaria.**

You: (translate)_____

Dr. Scalpi: Why? What symptoms do you have?

You: _____

Mara: **Siento falta de aire cuando camino, y además tengo muchos dolores de espalda y de columna.**

You: (translate)_____

Dr. Scalpi: What is your present weight?

You: (translate)_____

Mara: **Doscientas doce libras.**

You: (translate)_____

Dr. Scalpi: Do you exercise or play sports?

You: (translate)_____

Mara: **No, no hago ejercicio.**

You: (translate)_____

Dr. Scalpi: Do you smoke?

You: (translate)_____

Mara: **Sí, fumo un poco. Tres a cinco cigarrillos por día.**

You: (translate)_____

Dr. Scalpi: Do you have healthy eating habits?

You: (translate)_____

Mara: **Bueno, es que trabajo mucho y no como bien.**

You: (translate)_____

Dr. Scalpi: Do you urinate frequently? Do you get up to urinate at night?

You: (translate)_____

Mara: **Sí, orino varias veces en el día y de noche me levanto dos o tres veces.**

You: (translate)_____

Dr. Scalpi: OK, make an appointment in fifteen days. I need the results of the exams to give you a treatment plan.

You: (translate)_____

Mara: **Bien, doctor. Voy a hacer una cita en quince días entonces.**

You: (translate)_____

Dr. Scalpi: OK. See you in two weeks.

You: (translate)_____

Appendix 1

Especialidades Médicas

Medical Specialties

This lesson presents vocabulary you can use in the situations that arise in your own health care practice. You can use this specialized vocabulary in combination with the new skills you learned earlier in the book. Your handling and fluency of this material will greatly depend on how often and how much you practice!

Allergies and the Allergist

Alergias y el, la alergista

to animals: | **a animales:** | to insect bites | **a picadura de insectos**
animal dandruff | **caspa de animales** | to medicines: | **a medicinas:**
dust lice | **ácaros del polvo** | aspirin | **aspirina**
feathers | **plumas** | penicillin | **penicilina**
pets | **mascotas** | to perfumes | **a perfumes**
to dust | **al polvo** | to pollen: | **al polen:**
to food: | **a alimentos:** | hay fever | **fiebre del heno**
chocolate | **chocolate** | to other allergens: | **a otros alérgenos:**
lactose | **lactosa** | chemical products | **productos químicos**
milk | **leche** | mold | **moho**
peanuts, nuts | **maníes, nueces** | smoke | **humo**
seafood | **mariscos**
strawberries | **fresas**
tomatoes | **tomates**

(Please find vocabulary used to describe allergy symptoms among the other vocabulary lists in this appendix.)

Cardiology and the Cardiologist

Cardiología y el, la cardiólogo, -a

aneurysm	**aneurisma**	murmur	**soplo**
angina	**angina**	nitroglycerin	**nitroglicerina**
arteriosclerosis	**arterioesclerosis**	numbness and	**entumecimiento y**
bad cholesterol or LDL	**colesterol malo o LDL**	tingling	**hormigueo**
blocked artery	**arteria obstruída**	pacemaker	**marcapasos**
chest	**pecho**	palpitations	**palpitaciones**
good cholesterol	**colesterol bueno o HDL**	perspiration	**sudoraciones**
or HDL		shortness of breath	**falta de aire**
heart attack	**ataque cardíaco**	stroke, brain attack	**apoplejía, ataque o**
high cholesterol	**colesterol alto**		**derrame cerebral**
hypertension	**hipertensión arterial**	swelling	**hinchazones**
infarcts	**infartos**	tachycardia	**taquicardia**

Diabetes and Nutrition; the Nutritionist

Diabetes y nutrición; el, la nutricionista

calories	**calorías**	nutrition facts	**valores nutricionales**
carbohydrates	**carbohidratos,**	overweight	**sobrepeso**
	hidratos de carbono	physical activity	**actividad física**
change of habits	**cambio de hábitos**	pounds	**libras**
diet	**dieta**	proteins	**proteínas**
fat	**grasas**	(to) put on weight	**aumentar de peso**
glucose	**glucosa**	risk factors	**factores de riesgo**
hyperglycemia	**hiperglucemia**	smoking habit	**hábito de fumar**
insulin	**insulina**	sugar	**azúcar**
kilos	**kilos**	sugar substitute	**edulcorante**
lifestyle	**estilo de vida**	tryglicerids	**triglicéridos**
(to) lose weight	**bajar de peso**		

Dermatology and the Dermatologist

Dermatología y el, la dermatólogo, -a

acne	**acné**	pus	**pus**
blister	**ampolla**	rash	**erupción**
boil	**forúnculo**	skin	**piel**
cyst	**quiste**	spot	**mancha**
hives	**urticaria**	swelling	**hinchazón**
itching	**picazón**	varicose veins	**várices**
mole	**lunar**	wart	**verruga**
pimple	**grano**		

Please find extensive vocabulary for Food and Nutrition in Chapter 10.

Gastroenterology and the Gastroenterologist

Gastroenterología y el, la gastroenterólogo, -a

acidity	**acidez**	hiccups	**hipo**
bile	**bilis**	intestinal irritation	**irritación intestinal**
blood in stool	**sangre en el excremento, en las heces**	large intestine	**intestino grueso**
		laxatives	**laxantes**
colon	**colon**	liver	**hígado**
constipation	**estreñimiento**	nausea	**náuseas**
diarrhea	**diarrea**	pancreas	**páncreas**
flatulence, gas	**flatulencias, gases**	parasites	**parásitos**
gallbladder	**vesícula**	regurgitations	**regurgitaciones**
gallstone	**cálculo biliar, piedras en la vesícula**	small intestine	**intestino delgado**
		stomach	**estómago**
heartburn	**ardor en el estómago**	swallow	**tragar**
hemorrhoids	**hemorroides**	ulcers	**úlceras**
hepatitis	**hepatitis**	vomiting	**vómitos**

Gynecology and the Gynecologist

Ginecología y el, la Ginecólogo, -a

breasts	**las mamas, los senos**	menstrual cycle	**ciclo menstrual**
breast self-check	**autocontrol de las mamas o senos**	ovary	**ovario**
		ovulation	**ovulación**
contraceptive methods	**métodos anticonceptivos**	pap smear	**examen de papanicolao, pap**
cyst	**quiste**	sexual intercourse	**relaciones sexuales**
discharge	**secreción**	sterility	**esterilidad**
fallopian tubes	**trompas de falopio**	ultrasound (sonography, echography)	**ultrasonido (sonografía, ecografía)**
fertility	**fertilidad**		
hormones	**hormonas**		
menopause	**menopausia**		

Neurology and the Neurologist

Neurología y el, la neurólogo, -a

balance problems	**problemas con equilibrio**	numbness	**entumecimiento, adormecimiento**
blurred vision	**vista nublada**		
brain	**cerebro**	palsy, paralysis	**parálisis**
convulsions	**convulsiones**	restlessness	**agitación**
dizziness	**mareos**	spinal cord	**médula espinal**
epilepsy	**epilepsia**	stroke, brain attack	**apoplejía, ataque o derrame cerebral**
fainting spells	**desmayos**		
hemiplegia	**hemiplejia o hemiplejía**	stuttering	**tartamudeo**
lumbar puncture	**punción lumbar**	tingling	**hormigueo, cosquilleo**
nerves	**nervios**	tremors	**temblores**

Obstetrics and the Obstetrician

Obstetricia y el, la obstetra

amniotic liquid	**líquido amniótico**	midwife	**partera**
amniotic sac	**bolsa amniótica,**	placenta	**placenta**
	saco amniótico	pregnancy	**embarazo**
cervix	**cuello uterino**	pregnancy test	**examen de embarazo**
cesarean delivery	**parto por cesárea**	routine sonogram	**sonograma, ecografía**
contractions	**contracciones**		**de rutina**
delivery	**parto**	umbilical cord	**cordón umbilical**
delivery date	**fecha de parto**	uterus	**útero**
embryo	**embrión**	vaginal delivery	**parto vaginal**
fetus	**feto**	vitamin supplements	**suplementos vitamínicos**

Oncology and the Oncologist

Oncología y el, la oncólogo, -a

benign tumor	**tumor benigno**	leukemia	**leucemia**
biopsy	**biopsia**	lump	**bulto**
cancer:	**cáncer:**	lymph nodes	**ganglios linfáticos**
breast	**de mama, de seno**	malignant tumor	**tumor maligno**
colon	**de colon**	mammography	**mamografía**
lung	**de pulmón**	mastectomy	**mastectomía**
prostate	**de próstata**	metastasis	**metástasis**
skin	**de piel**	node	**nódulo, ganglio**
stomach	**de estómago**	radiation	**radiación**
chemotherapy	**quimioterapia**		

Ophthalmology and the Ophthalmologist

Oftalmología y el, la oftalmólogo, -a

blurred vision	**visión borrosa**	iris	**iris**
cataracts	**cataratas**	lacrimal gland	**glándula lagrimal**
conjunctivitis	**conjuntivitis**	pupil	**pupila**
dilation of the pupil	**dilatación de pupila**	redness in the eyes	**ojos rojos, ojos**
eye, eyes	**ojo, ojos**		**colorados**
eye drops	**gotas para los ojos**	retinal detachment	**desprendimiento**
eyelash	**pestaña**		**de retina**
eyelid	**párpado**	sclera	**esclerótica**
glasses	**anteojos**	sty	**orzuelo**

Orthopedics and the Orthopedist; Podiatry and the Podiatrist

Ortopedia y el, la ortopedista, el, la especialista en ortopedia; podiatría y el, la podiatra, el, la especialista en podiatría

ankle	**tobillo**	nape (of the neck)	**nuca**
arm	**brazo**	neck	**cuello**
back	**espalda**	osteoporosis	**osteoporosis**
bones	**huesos**	palm	**palma**
calf	**pantorrilla**	patella	**rótula**
clavicle	**clavícula**	rheumatism	**reumatismo**
elbow	**codo**	ribs	**costillas**
fingers	**dedos, dedos de la mano**	scapula	**omóplato**
foot	**pie**	spine	**columna, espina vertebral**
forearm	**antebrazo**		
hand	**mano**	sternum	**esternón**
heel	**talón**	thigh	**muslo**
joints	**articulaciones**	tissues	**tejidos**
leg	**pierna**	toes	**dedos del pie**
ligaments	**ligamentos**	wrist	**muñeca**
muscles	**músculos**		

Otolaryngology and the Otolaryngologist

Otolaringología y el, la otolaringólogo, -a

difficulty breathing	**dificultad para respirar**	otitis	**otitis**
ear	**oído**	sinusitis	**sinusitis**
glottis	**glotis**	specialist in voice treatment	**foniatra**
inflamed tonsils	**amígdalas inflamadas**		
head	**cabeza**	tongue	**lengua**
lobule	**lóbulo**	throat	**garganta**
mouth	**boca**	tonsilitis	**amigdalitis**
nose	**nariz**	vocal cords	**cuerdas vocales**

Pediatrics and the Pediatrician

Pediatría y el, la pediatra

baby	**bebé**
bath	**baño**
bathtub	**bañera**
breastfeeding:	**amamantamiento:**
to breastfeed	**amamantar, dar el pecho, dar de mamar, dar "la teta"**
child	**niño, -a**
cold	**catarro, resfrío, resfriado**
colic	**cólico**
cough	**tos**
diaper:	**pañal:**
diaper rash	**dermatitis del pañal**
eructation, belch	**eructo, "provechito"**
fever	**fiebre**
gas	**gases**
growth	**crecimiento**
hiccups	**hipo**
milk:	**leche:**
cow's	**de vaca**
lactose free	**sin lactosa**
maternal	**materna**
soy	**de soja**
navel, umbilicus	**ombligo**
nipple	**pezón**
nourishment	**nutrición, alimentación**
nursing bottle	**biberón, mamadera**
pacifier	**chupete**
teether	**mordillo**
teething	**dentición**
temperature	**temperatura**
throat (swab) culture	**cultivo (por hisopado) de garganta**
vaccines:	**vacunas:**
DTP:	**DTP:**
(diphteria/tetanus/pertussis)	**(difteria/tétanos/tos convulsa)**
haemophilus influenzae B	**hemófilo influenza B**
hepatitis A, hepatitis B	**hepatitis A, hepatitis B**
MMR:	**triple viral/MMR:**
(measles/mumps/rubella)	**(sarampión/paperas/rubeola)**
poliomyelitis	**poliomielitis**
tuberculosis	**tuberculosis**
varicella, chicken pox	**varicela**
weight	**peso**
weaning	**destete**

Psychiatry and the Psychiatrist; Psychology and the Psychologist

Psiquiatría y el, la psiquiatra; psicología y el, la psicólogo, -a

addictions	**adicciones**	loss of interest	**pérdida de interés**
alcoholism	**alcoholismo**	mood changes	**cambios de humor**
anxiety	**ansiedad**	nightmares	**pesadillas**
behavior changes	**cambios de conducta**	panic attacks	**ataques de pánico**
depression	**depresión**	personality areas	**áreas de la personalidad**
dreams	**sueños**	relation with peers	**relación con pares**
drug addiction	**drogadicción**	relationship problems	**problemas de pareja**
emotional disorders	**trastornos emocionales**		
fatigue	**fatiga**	respect	**respeto**
guilt feelings	**sentimientos de culpa**	self-esteem	**autoestima**
insomnia	**insomnio**	social behavior	**comportamiento social**

Respiratory Care; the Respiratory Care Specialist

Cuidados respiratorios; el, la especialista en afecciones respiratorias

asthma, asthma attack	**asma, ataque de asma**	phlegmy cough	**tos con flema**
		pneumonia	**pulmonía, neumonía**
bacteria	**bacteria**	smoker	**fumador**
bronchus, bronchi	**bronquio, bronquios**	secondhand smoke	**humo de segunda mano**
chronic bronchitis	**bronquitis crónica**	secondhand smoker	**fumador pasivo o de segunda mano**
colds	**resfríos**		
cough	**tos**	sniffle	**catarro nasal**
dry cough	**tos seca**	snoring	**respiración con ronquido**
emphysema	**enfisema**	trachea	**tráquea**
flu	**gripe**	virus	**virus**
loud respiration	**respiración ruidosa**	wheezing	**respiración sibilante**
lungs	**pulmones**		

Special Needs

Necesidades especiales

autism	**autismo**	special needs	**necesidades especiales**
disabilities, disabled	**discapacidades, discapacitado**	special school	**escuela especial**
		speech and language impairments	**trastornos del habla y lenguaje**
hearing impairment	**incapacidad auditiva**		
hearing aids	**audífonos**	speech and language therapist	**terapista del habla y del lenguaje**
home health care	**cuidado en el hogar**		
household assistance	**ayuda doméstica**	stuttering	**tartamudez**
limited ability	**habilidad limitada**	visual impairment	**incapacidad visual**
occupational therapy workshops	**talleres de terapia ocupacional**	(power) wheelchair	**silla de ruedas (motorizada)**
physical activity	**actividad física**		
sign language	**idioma de señas**		

Urology and the Urologist

Urología y el, la urólogo, -a

bladder	**vejiga**	penis	**pene**
blood in stool	**sangre en el excremento, en las heces**	prostate	**próstata**
		scrotum	**escroto**
blood in urine	**sangre en la orina**	sexual intercourse	**relaciones sexuales**
burning when urinating	**ardor al orinar**	testicles	**testículos**
		urethra	**uretra**
discharge	**secreción**	urinary infection	**infección urinaria**
enuresis	**enuresis**	venereal diseases	**enfermedades venéreas**
itching	**picazón**		
kidneys	**riñones**		

Appendix 2

Verb References

In Spanish, the pronoun *usted* is used to address "you" in formal situations. For "you" in informal situations, such as when speaking to a young child or friend, the pronoun *tú* is used. To refer to the plural "you" in Spanish, we use *ustedes*.

In this section, you'll find verb conjugations for commonly used verbs. After each verb, you can build your skills by writing sample sentences based on the examples.

The Simple Present Tense

ser (to be)

yo	I	**soy**	am
tú	you (informal)	**eres**	are
usted, él, ella	you (formal), he, she	**es**	are, is
nosotros	we	**somos**	are
ustedes	you	**son**	are
ellos, ellas	they	**son**	are

For example:
Yo <u>soy</u> la Dra. Palacios. (Chapter 1)   I am Dr. Palacios.
¿Cuál <u>es</u> su seguro médico? (Chapter 3)   What is your medical insurance?
Carlos y Andrea <u>son</u> asociados médicos.   Carlos and Andrea are physician assistants.
Nosotros <u>somos</u> turistas.   We are tourists.

estar (to be)

The verb *estar* is used to indicate location or mood.

yo	I	**estoy**	am
tú	you (informal)	**estás**	are
usted, él, ella	you (formal), he, she	**está**	are, is
nosotros	we	**estamos**	are
ustedes	you	**están**	are
ellos, ellas	they	**están**	are

For example:
El Dr. Francisco Olleros <u>está</u> en la sala de partos. (Chapter 6)
Dr. Francisco Olleros is in the delivery room.
<u>Estoy</u> muy preocupado. (Chapter 6)
I am very worried.
Nosotros <u>estamos</u> aquí desde las cinco de la tarde.
We are here since 5 P.M.

Conjugation of Regular Verbs

All verbs in Spanish end in *-ar, -er,* or *-ir.* To conjugate a regular verb you drop the *-ar, -er,* or *-ir* infinitive ending and add the appropriate verb ending.

Verbs Ending in *-ar*

traba<u>jar</u> (to work)

yo	I	**trabaj<u>o</u>**	work
tú	you (informal)	**trabaj<u>as</u>**	work
usted, él, ella	you (formal), he, she	**trabaj<u>a</u>**	work, works
nosotros	we	**trabaj<u>amos</u>**	work
ustedes	you	**trabaj<u>an</u>**	work
ellos, ellas	they	**trabaj<u>an</u>**	work

Observe the conjugation of another regular verb ending in *-ar, hablar* (to speak): *yo habl<u>o</u>, tú habl<u>as</u>, usted/él/ella habl<u>a</u>, nosotros habl<u>amos</u>, ustedes habl<u>an</u>, ellos habl<u>an</u>.*

Can you try with *cami<u>nar</u>* (to walk) and *u<u>sar</u>* (to use)? Then complete the following sentences by putting verbs ending in *-ar* in the correct form. You can also try making up new sentences afterwards! (recommended after Chapter 5)

Nosotros (a)_____(estudiar/study) **mucho.**

Juana y Ana (b)_____(cenar/eat dinner) **a las nueve de la noche.**

¿Dónde (c)_____ (trabajar) **tú?**

El doctor (d)_____ (analizar/analyze) **todos los exámenes médicos de sus pacientes.**

Yo (e)_____ (hablar) **inglés y un poco de español.**

Verbs Ending in *-er*

com<u>er</u> (to eat)

yo	I	**com<u>o</u>**	eat
tú	you (informal)	**com<u>es</u>**	eat
usted, él, ella	you (formal), he, she	**com<u>e</u>**	eat, eats
nosotros	we	**com<u>emos</u>**	eat
ustedes	you	**com<u>en</u>**	eat
ellos, ellas	they	**com<u>en</u>**	eat

Observe the conjugation of another regular verb ending in *-er, leer* (to read): *yo le<u>o</u>, tú le<u>es</u>, usted/él/ella le<u>e</u>, nosotros le<u>emos</u>, ustedes le<u>en</u>, ellos le<u>en</u>.*

Can you try with *be<u>ber</u>* (to drink) and *rom<u>per</u>* (to break)? Then complete the following sentences by putting the verbs ending in *-er* in the correct form. You can also try making up new sentences afterwards! (recommended after Chapter 5)

El paciente López no (a)_____(comer) **vegetales.**

Yo (b)_____ (comer) **todos los días a las 12:30 P.M.**

El doctor (c) _____ (leer) los informes de sus pacientes todas las mañanas.

Juan (d) _____ (beber) mucho alcohol.

¿Usted (e) _____ (beber) mucho alcohol?

Verbs Ending in *-ir*

vivir (to live)

yo	I	viv**o**	live
tú	you (informal)	viv**es**	live
usted, él, ella	you (formal), he, she	viv**e**	live, lives
nosotros	we	viv**imos**	live
ustedes	you	viv**en**	live
ellos, ellas	they	viv**en**	live

Observe the conjugation of another regular verb ending in *-ir*, *insistir* (to insist): *yo insist**o**, tú insist**es**, usted/él/ella insist**e**, nosotros insist**imos**, ustedes insist**en**, ellos insist**en***.

Can you try with *decidir* (to decide) and *escribir* (to write)? Then complete the following sentences by putting the verbs ending in *-ir* in the correct form. (recommended after Chapter 5)

El Dr. Puentes (a)_____(insistir) con el diagnóstico.

¿Dónde (b)_____ (vivir) ustedes?

Juan y yo (c) _____ (insistir) con adoptar un bebé.

¿Usted (d)_____ (vivir) aquí?

María les (e)_____ (escribir) a sus hijos todos los días.

Conjugation of Irregular Verbs

Some verbs in Spanish don't follow the same conjugation pattern as regular verbs. See the conjugation of some frequently used irregular verbs:

tener (to have)

yo	I	tengo	have
tú	you (informal)	tienes	have
usted, él, ella	you (formal), he, she	tiene	have, has
nosotros	we	tenemos	have
ustedes	you	tienen	have
ellos, ellas	they	tienen	have

For example:
El Dr. Johnson <u>tiene</u> un consultorio en Philadelphia. (Chapter 4)
Dr. Johnson has an office in Philadelphia.
María y Pedro <u>tienen</u> dos hijos. (Chapter 4)
María and Pedro have two children.
Doctor, <u>tengo</u> dolores de cabeza muy frecuentes. (Chapter 2)
Doctor, I have very frequent headaches.

Many verbs in Spanish that end in *-tener* are conjugated the same way as *tener.* For example: *obtener* (to get), *contener* (to contain), *retener* (to retain).

For example:

¿**Doctor, esta medicina <u>contiene</u> paracetamol?**		Doctor, does this medicine contain paracetamol?	
¿**Qué resultados <u>obtengo</u> haciéndolo?**		What results do I get by doing so?	

hacer (to do, to make)

yo	I	hago	make
tú	you (informal)	haces	make
usted, él, ella	you (formal), he, she	hace	make, makes
nosotros	we	hacemos	make
ustedes	you	hacen	make
ellos, ellas	they	hacen	make

For example:

No, yo no <u>hago</u> ejercicio físico regularmente.
No, I don't do physical exercise regularly.
Laura <u>hace</u> una consulta con el ginecólogo todos los años.
Laura has a consultation with the gynecologist every year.

Verbs ending with *-acer* are conjugated in the same way as *hacer,* as for example *satisfacer* (to satisfy):

El Dr. Suárez <u>satisface</u> a sus pacientes respondiendo a todas sus preguntas.
Dr. Suárez satisfies his patients by answering all their questions.

almorzar (to have lunch)

yo	I	almuerzo	have lunch
tú	you (informal)	almuerzas	have lunch
usted, él, ella	you (formal), he, she	almuerza	have, has lunch
nosotros	we	almorzamos	have lunch
ustedes	you	almuerzan	have lunch
ellos, ellas	they	almuerzan	have lunch

Note also that the verb *acostarse* (to lay down) follows this same conjugation.

For example:
Tengo dolor por la noche cuando me <u>acuesto</u>. (Chapter 9)
I have pain at night when I lie down.

Refer to Chapter 9, page 91, to revisit reflexive verbs.

ir (to go)

yo	I	voy	go
tú	you (informal)	vas	go
usted, él, ella	you (formal), he, she	va	go, goes
nosotros	we	vamos	go
ustedes	you	van	go
ellos, ellas	they	van	go

For example:

Yo <u>voy</u> a la oficina a las ocho y media de la mañana. (Chapter 10)
I go to the office at eight thirty in the morning.
Los sábados mi familia y yo <u>vamos</u> a la playa.
On Saturdays, my family and I go to the beach.
<u>Vamos a hacer</u> un electrocardiograma. (Chapters 2 and 3, future form)
We are going to do an EKG.

Notice that the "going to" future form is made up the conjugated form of the verb *ir* + the preposition *a* + the infinitive verb. (Refer to the Grammar in Use section, Chapters 2 and 3, pages 11 and 26, for more information.)

salir (to go out)

yo	I	**salgo**	go out
tú	you (informal)	**sales**	go out
usted, él, ella	you (formal), he, she	**sale**	go, goes out
nosotros	we	**salimos**	go out
ustedes	you	**salen**	go out
ellos, ellas	they	**salen**	go out

For example:

Yo <u>salgo</u> todos los fines de semana.   I go out every weekend.
<u>Salimos</u> del trabajo a las seis de la tarde.   We leave work at 6 P.M.

decir (to say)

yo	I	**digo**	say
tú	you (informal)	**dices**	say
usted, él, ella	you (formal), he, she	**dice**	say, says
nosotros	we	**decimos**	say
ustedes	you	**dicen**	say
ellos, ellas	they	**dicen**	say

For example:

El paciente Pedro Martello <u>dice</u> que no recuerda nada.
Patient Pedro Martello says he does not remember anything.

dormir (to sleep)

yo	I	**duermo**	sleep
tú	you (informal)	**duermes**	sleep
usted, él, ella	you (formal), he, she	**duerme**	sleep, sleeps
nosotros	we	**dormimos**	sleep
ustedes	you	**duermen**	sleep
ellos, ellas	they	**duermen**	sleep

For example:

¿Cuántas horas <u>duerme</u> (usted) por día? (Chapter 11)
How many hours do you sleep per day?

The Present Continuous Tense: Actions Happening NOW!

This tense form is formed from *estar* (conjugated) + main verb ending in *-ando, -iendo*. It is similar to the present continuous **to be + -ing** form in English.

Verbs Ending in *-ar*

These verbs take the *-ando* ending.

trabajar (to work) These verbs take the *-ando* ending.

yo	I	**estoy trabajando**	am working
tú	you (informal)	**estás trabajando**	are working
usted, él, ella	you (formal), he, she	**está trabajando**	are, is working
nosotros	we	**estamos trabajando**	are working
ustedes	you	**están trabajando**	are working
ellos, ellas	they	**están trabajando**	are working

More verbs:

tomar (to drink, to take): **tomando**   **examinar** (to examine): **examinando**
investigar (to investigate): **investigando**   **estudiar** (to study): **estudiando**

> For example:
> **Nosotros estamos investigando el caso.**
> We are investigating the case.
> **El Dr. Fernández está examinando al paciente.**
> Dr. Fernández is examining the patient.

Verbs Ending in *-er* and *-ir*

These verbs take the *-iendo* ending.

comer (to eat)

yo	I	**estoy comiendo**	am eating
tú	you (informal)	**estás comiendo**	are eating
usted, él, ella	you (formal), he, she	**está comiendo**	are, is eating
nosotros	we	**estamos comiendo**	are eating
ustedes	you	**están comiendo**	are eating
ellos, ellas	they	**están comiendo**	are eating

More verbs:

beber (to drink): **bebiendo**   decidir (to decide): **decidiendo**
hacer (to do, make): **haciendo**   insistir (to insist): **insistiendo**
romper (to break): **rompiendo**   asistir (to assist): **asistiendo**

> For example:
> **(Nosotros) Estamos haciendo todo lo posible.**   We are doing everything possible.
> **La enfermera está asistiendo al paciente.**   The nurse is assisting the patient.

The Simple Past Tense

ser (to be)

yo	I	**fui**	was
tú	you (informal)	**fuiste**	were
usted, él, ella	you (formal), he, she	**fue**	were, was
nosotros	we	**fuimos**	were
ustedes	you	**fueron**	were
ellos, ellas	they	**fueron**	were

For example:
(Yo) no <u>fui</u> muy claro con mi pregunta.   I wasn't very clear with my question.
María <u>fue</u> muy precisa.   María was very precise.

estar (to be)

yo	I	**estuve**	was
tú	you (informal)	**estuviste**	were
usted, el, ella	you (formal), he, she	**estuvo**	were, was
nosotros	we	**estuvimos**	were
ustedes	you	**estuvieron**	were
ellos, ellas	they	**estuvieron**	were

For example:
Yo <u>estuve</u> aquí la semana pasada.
I was here last week.
Los técnicos <u>estuvieron</u> en un curso de capacitación la semana pasada.
The technicians were in a training course last week.

Let's practice! Can you put the following verbs into their correct form? Remember that *estar* is used to indicate mood or location.

Ayer nosotros (a)_____(estar) aquí todo el día.

La hija de Manuela (b)_____ (estar) presente en la consulta.

La reunión (c)_____ (ser) muy satisfactoria.

La doctora (d)_____ (ser) muy directa durante la conversación.

El paciente Juárez (e) _____ (estar) muy nervioso durante la entrevista.

Regular Verbs

Verbs Ending in -ar

informar (to inform)

yo	I	**informé**	informed
tú	you (informal)	**informaste**	informed
usted, él, ella	you (formal), he, she	**informó**	informed
nosotros	we	**informamos**	informed
ustedes	you	**informaron**	informed
ellos, ellas	they	**informaron**	informed

Here is another *-ar* verb conjugated in the simple past tense: *esperar* (to wait): *yo esperé, tú esperaste, usted/él/ella esperó, nosotros esperamos, ustedes esperaron, ellos esperaron.*

Can you try to conjugate *amar* (to love) and *entrar* (to enter) in the simple past? Then make up sentences with the verbs.

> For example:
> **(Nosotros) Trabajamos mucho ayer.**
> We worked a lot yesterday.
> **El paciente entró a la sala de operaciones muy tranquilo.**
> The patient entered the operation room very calmly.

Verbs Ending in -er and -ir

atender (to look after)

yo	I	**atendí**	looked after
tú	you (informal)	**atendiste**	looked after
usted, él, ella	you (formal), he, she	**atendió**	looked after
nosotros	we	**atendimos**	looked after
ustedes	you	**atendieron**	looked after
ellos, ellas	they	**atendieron**	looked after

More verbs:

comer (to eat): *yo comí, tú comiste, usted/él/ella comió, nosotros comimos, ustedes comieron, ellos comieron*

decidir (to decide): *yo decidí, tú decidiste, usted/él/ella decidió, nosotros decidimos, ustedes decidieron, ellos decidieron*

Can you try to form sentences with *nacer* (to be born), *morder* (to bite), and *partir* (to leave, to depart)?

> For example:
> **Me mordió un perro.**   A dog bit me.
> **¿Qué decidieron (ustedes)?**   What did you decide?

Let's practice! Can you conjugate the following verbs in the past tense?

(recommended after Chapter 11)

La enfermera (a)_____ (asistir) a todos sus pacientes.

Los pacientes (b)_____ (esperar) dos horas para consultar al doctor.

El paciente López no (c)_____ **(comer) la comida.**

Doctor, nosotros (d)_____ **(decidir) adoptar un hijo.**

Doctor, (yo) ya (e)_____ **(tomar) una decisión.**

Irregular Verbs

Some irregular verbs do not differ much from regular verbs in their conjugation, others do. Let's consider the verbs that are conjugated quite differently than regular verbs and that you may often need.

tener (to have)

yo	I	tuve	had
tú	you (informal)	tuviste	had
usted, él, ella	you (formal), he, she	tuvo	had
nosotros	we	tuvimos	had
ustedes	you	tuvieron	had
ellos, ellas	they	tuvieron	had

> For example:
> **Yo <u>tuve</u> una erupción el mes pasado.**   I had a rash last month.
> **La Sra. Galdi <u>tuvo</u> un bebé la semana pasada.**   Mrs. Galdi had a baby last week.
> **Nosotros <u>tuvimos</u> un examen el lunes pasado.**   We had an exam last Monday.

decir (to tell, to say)

yo	I	dije	said
tú	you (informal)	dijiste	said
usted, él, ella	you (formal), he, she	dijo	said
nosotros	we	dijimos	said
ustedes	you	dijeron	said
ellos, ellas	they	dijeron	said

> For example:
> **El Dr. Pérez me <u>dijo</u> que usted tuvo algunas complicaciones.**
> Dr. Pérez told me that you had some complications.
> **(Yo) Le <u>dije</u> a la paciente que espere aquí.**
> I told the patient to wait here.

ir (to go)

yo	I	fui	went
tú	you (informal)	fuiste	went
usted, él, ella	you (formal), he, she	fue	went
nosotros	we	fuimos	went
ustedes	you	fueron	went
ellos, ellas	they	fueron	went

> For example:
> **Mi madre <u>fue</u> al consultorio del Dr. Frutos.**
> My mother went to Dr. Frutos's office.
> **Ayer (yo) <u>fui</u> al hospital para un chequeo general.**
> Yesterday I went to the hospital for a general examination.

hacer (to make, to do)

yo	I	**hice**	did, made
tú	you (informal)	**hiciste**	did, made
usted, él, ella	you (formal), he, she	**hizo**	did, made
nosotros	we	**hicimos**	did, made
ustedes	you	**hicieron**	did, made
ellos, ellas	they	**hicieron**	did, made

For example:

¿Qué <u>hicieron</u> (ustedes) en la convención?   What did you do at the convention?

¿Qué <u>hizo</u> el paciente Vargas finalmente?   What did patient Vargas finally do?

Let's practice! Can you conjugate the following verbs in the past tense?

(recommended after Chapter 11)

Nosotros (a)_____ **(ir) al hospital a las seis de la mañana.**

El doctor (b)_____ **(decir) que tengo que comer sin sal.**

Doctor, esta mañana mi hijo (c)_____ **(tener) muchos dolores abdominales.**

¿Qué (d)_____ **(hacer) tú el fin de semana?**

Su hijo ya (e)_____ **(tener) varicela, ¿verdad?**

Useful Past Tense Time References

ayer	yesterday
anteayer	the day before yesterday
pasado, -a	last
la semana <u>pasada</u>	<u>last</u> week
el martes <u>pasado</u>	<u>last</u> Tuesday
hace	ago
<u>hace</u> dos días	two days <u>ago</u>
<u>hace</u> un año	a year <u>ago</u>
atrás	ago
tres meses <u>atrás</u>	three months <u>ago</u>

The Present Perfect Tense

This tense is introduced in Chapter 11, to provide you with some basic tools you may need to understand and incorporate to your knowledge of the language. The present perfect tense in Spanish is made up by the conjugated form of the auxiliary verb **haber** (equivalent to the auxiliary verb "to have" in English), plus the past participle of the main verb.

The participle of regular verbs ending in -*ar* will end in -*ado*.

For example: *inform**ar*** (to inform), *inform**ado*** (participle, informed)

yo	I	**he** inform**ado**	have informed
tú	you (informal)	**has** inform**ado**	have informed
usted, él, ella	you (formal), he, she	**ha** inform**ado**	have, has informed
nosotros	we	**hemos** inform**ado**	have informed
ustedes	you	**han** inform**ado**	have informed
ellos, ellas	they	**han** inform**ado**	have informed

For example:
Ya me han informado acerca de los riesgos quirúrgicos.
They <u>have</u> already <u>informed</u> me about the surgical risks.

The participle of regular verbs ending in -*er* and -*ir* will end in -*ido*.

For example: *com**er*** (to eat), *com**ido*** (participle, eaten); *refer**ir*** (to refer), *refer**ido*** (participle, referred)

yo	I	**he** refer**ido**	have referred
tú	you (informal)	**has** refer**ido**	have referred
usted, él, ella	you (formal), he, she	**ha** refer**ido**	have, has referred
nosotros	we	**hemos** refer**ido**	have referred
ustedes	you	**han** refer**ido**	have referred
ellos, ellas	they	**han** refer**ido**	have referred

For example:
Los pacientes no han comido la cena aún.
The patients <u>have</u> not <u>eaten</u> their dinner yet.
Mi médico general me ha referido a un cardiólogo.
My general physician <u>has referred</u> me to a cardiologist.

Let's practice! Can you conjugate the following verbs in the present perfect tense?

(recommended after Chapter 11)

El nutricionista me (a)_____ **(indicar) una dieta muy estricta.**

Mi médico general me (b)_____ **(referir) a un ginecólogo.**

Doctor, (c)_____ **(seguir) todas sus recomendaciones.**

La enfermera me (d)_____ **(recomendar) reposo en cama.**

Los pacientes no (e) _____ **(comer) el postre hoy.**

Verb conjugation in Spanish is not a simple task! Hopefully, you now have a general idea of the basics. Consult a Spanish grammar book or web site for further practice.

Appendix 3

Dialog Comprehension and Written Exercises Answer Key

Chapter 1
Dialog Comprehension

Dr. Valle and Dr. Robinson are meeting for the first time. They are shaking hands.

Written Exercises

1. (a) Buenos días.
   (b) Soy el paciente.
   (c) Un placer (mucho gusto).
2. (a) Soy la enfermera Beatriz Nuñez, mucho gusto.
   (b) Soy el asociado médico Pedro Bolaños, mucho gusto.
   (c) Soy el anestesista Luis Pedras, mucho gusto.
3. Just try your best!

Chapter 2
Dialog Comprehension

El paciente es Pedro López.
The patient is from Venezuela.
He works in a supermarket.

Written Exercises

1. Just practice!
2. (a) Cuál/(3)
   (b) Dónde/(1)
   (c) dónde/(5)
   (d) Cuál/(4)
   (e) Cuál/(2)
3. (a) Cuál
   (b) Dónde
   (c) Dónde
   (d) Dónde
   (e) Cuánto hace
4. argentina, alemana, brasileña, chilena, colombiana, cubana, salvadoreña, estadounidense, americana, francesa, griega, hondureña, inglesa, nicaragüense, peruana, puertorriqueña, venezolana
5. Just practice!
6. (a) dos meses
   (b) treinta y nueve semanas
   (c) diez años
   (d) six months
   (e) fifteen days
   (f) three years

Chapter 3
Dialog Comprehension

Benito Gómez es el nombre del paciente.
Seguro social means social security.
"Salud de la Familia" es su seguro médico.
7100 "SW" 126 "Street" es su domicilio.

Written Exercises

1. (a) 3
   (b) 4
   (c) 1
   (d) 6
   (e) 2
   (f) 5
2. (a) nombre
   (b) Cuál
   (c) es
   (d) (número de) seguro social
   (e) ¿Cuál es el motivo de la consulta?/¿Qué le pasa?
3. (a) Cuál es
   (b) Qué
   (c) caí
   (d) domicilio
   (e) Cuál es
   (f) Cuál es
   (g) Soy
   (h) Es
   (i) caí
   (j) hacer

Chapter 4
Dialog Comprehension

El Dr. Juan Luppi trabaja en el Hospital General, en Chile.
La Dra. Akiko Sato es dermatóloga.
Marta Vallesteros es asociado médico.
El Dr. Michel Spencer es hematólogo.

Written Exercises

1. (a) Pedro Palos es ginecólogo. (Él) Es de Méjico. (Él) Trabaja en un hospital en Veracruz. (Él) Es casado y tiene tres hijos.
   (b) María Lovetto es cardióloga. (Ella) Es de Brasil. (Ella) Trabaja en un hospital en Río de Janeiro. (Ella) Es soltera.

2. (a) pediatra
   (b) hospital
   (c) Coral Gables
   (d) Sí, tiene un consultorio en South Miami, y otro en Miami Beach.
3. Just write! Enjoy your paragraphs!
4. Write about yourself.

Chapter 5
Dialog Comprehension

La paciente se llama Kem Khatkjial.
Khatkjial es el apellido de la paciente.
Medical Plan es el seguro médico de la paciente.

Written Exercises

1. (a) Cuál   (c) Cuál
   (b) cincuenta y ocho   (d) edad
2. (a) tiene
   (b) treinta y dos años
   (c) Cuántos años tiene
   (d) Pedro tiene veinticuatro
   (e) Cuántos años tiene
   (f) Luis tiene cuarenta y seis años.
   (g) Cuántos años tiene
   (h) Silvia tiene cincuenta años.
   (i) ¿Cuántos años tiene
   (j) Carmen tiene sesenta y siete años.
3. Check numbers in the Vocabulary Practice section.
4. Check numbers in the Vocabulary Practice section.
5. (a) Tengo cita con el doctor a las dos de la tarde.
   (b) Tengo cita con el doctor a las seis de la tarde.
   (c) Tengo cita con el doctor a las nueve de la mañana.
   (d) Tengo cita con el doctor a las diez de la mañana.
   (e) Tengo cita con el doctor a las siete de la tarde.
6. (a) ocho y veinticinco   (e) una y cuarto, quince
   (b) siete y cuarenta   (f) seis y cincuenta y cinco
   (c) nueve y cincuenta
   (d) dos y media
7. (a) ¿Qué hora es?   (j) ¿Qué hora es?
   (b) Son las ocho y treinta.   (k) Es la una y treinta.
   (c) Son las ocho y media.   (l) Es la una y media.
   (d) ¿Qué hora es?   (m) ¿Qué hora es?
   (e) Son las diez y quince.   (n) Son las siete y treinta y cinco.
   (f) Son las diez y cuarto.
   (g) ¿Qué hora es?   (o) Son las ocho menos veinticinco.
   (h) Son las tres y cuarenta y cinco.
   (i) Son las cuatro menos cuarto.
8. (a) El paciente Leonardo Mares tiene cuarenta y siete años.
   (b) Él tiene antecedentes de hipertensión, glucemia, resfríos y gripes frecuentes y cálculos en la vesícula.
   (c) Va a hacerse los análisis de sangre y orina el lunes.
   (d) Tiene cita para su radiografía de tórax el martes a las ocho y cuarto de la mañana.

(e) El martes va a realizarse un electrocardiograma.
(f) Tiene cita con el cardiólogo el miércoles.
(g) Va a tener el resultado de los análisis de sangre y orina el miércoles.
(h) El jueves va a realizarse una ecografía de vesícula.
(i) Tiene cita con el Dr. Vázquez el viernes a las siete y veinte de la noche.
(j) El Dr. Vázquez es médico general.

Chapters 1 to 5 Self-Check Exercise

1. (a) La   2. (a) Cuál
   (b) El   (b) dónde
   (c) la   (c) Cuánto
   (d) la   (d) Cuándo
   (e) el; la   (e) qué
3. (a) trescientos sesenta y cinco
   (b) cuatro millones quinientos mil
   (c) un millón ochocientos mil
   (d) treinta
   (e) dos mil trescientos cincuenta y seis
4. (a) nurse   5. (a) asociado médico
   (b) reason   (b) estómago
   (c) left arm   (c) piernas
   (d) cardiologist   (d) médico, médica
   (e) physician's office (e) paciente
6. soy; trabaja; vivo; tiene; habla

Chapter 6
Dialog Comprehension

El paciente necesita ir al laboratorio y a la sala de radiología.
El paciente González necesita hacerse una radiografía.
La recepcionista se llama María.

Written Exercises

1. (a) La Sra. Martínez está en la sala de maternidad.
   (b) La sala de emergencias está en el primer piso.
   (c) La Sra. Vásquez está en la sala de espera.
   (d) La familia Prieto está en la sala de pediatría.
   (e) El departamento de pediatría está en el segundo piso.
   (f) La sala de espera está en el primer piso.
2. (a) Dónde   (e) Dónde
   (b) Dónde   (f) Cómo
   (c) Cómo   (g) Dónde
   (d) Cómo

Role-Playing Exercise, Listening Comprehension Activity

his left ankle; an accident at work; in construction; a fracture and cast; six weeks

Chapter 7
Dialog Comprehension

María has stomachaches.
The general physician refers María to a gastroenterologist.

Written Exercises

1. (a) Mi paciente se llama Manuel Cadenas. Su esposa se llama Delia.
   (b) Mi paciente se llama Beatriz Contreras. Su hijo se llama Mauricio.
   (c) Mi paciente se llama Carlos Valler. Su madre se llama Eugenia.
2. (a) mi
   (b) su
   (c) Mi
   (d) su
   (e) Mi
3. (a) lo
   (b) -lo
   (c) la
   (d) -la
   (e) -lo
4. (a) Mr. González, I am going to prescribe you a cough syrup.
   (b) Mrs. Pérez, the nutritionist is going to indicate a diet for you.
   (c) Mr. Ramírez, I am going to prescribe you a medicine for your pain.
   (d) Mrs. Suárez, we are going to take an X-ray of your hip.
5. novia/girlfriend   hermana/sister
   suegra/mother-in-law   abuela/grandmother
   amigo/friend   hija/daughter
   cuñado/brother-in-law   sobrino/nephew
   madre/mother   sobrina/niece
6. Write as many sentences as you can!

Chapter 8
Dialog Comprehension

El apellido del paciente es Pérez.
El Sr. Pérez está en el hospital.
El Dr. Céspedes está en su trabajo, en el hospital.

Written Exercises

1. Just think of them and write!
2. (a) es
   (b) tiene
   (c) es
   (d) tiene
   (e) Tiene
   (f) es
   (g) es
   (h) tiene
3. Enjoy the experience of describing a person you admire! Just write and practice!

Chapter 9
Dialog Comprehension

El Sr. García tiene dolor en el pecho.
Esta no es la primera visita del Sr. Pérez al centro ortopédico. (Es su segunda visita.)
The doctor prescribed a different dose of the same anti-inflammatory.

Written Exercises

1. (a) este antiinflamatorio
   (b) estas medicinas
   (c) este descongestivo nasal
   (d) este jarabe
   (e) estas píldoras anticonceptivas
   (f) este antibiótico
   (g) esta tableta
2. (a) Tome estas píldoras cada ocho horas.
   (b) Tome este antiinflamatorio con las comidas.
   (c) Tome esta medicina antes de las comidas.
   (d) Tome este jarabe para la tos por la mañana.
   (e) Tome estas píldoras anticonceptivas todos los días.
   (f) Tome estas cápsulas después de las comidas.
   (g) Tome estos antiácidos antes de las comidas.
3. (a) Me duelen los ojos.
   (b) Me duele la cabeza.
   (c) Me duelen las caderas.
   (d) Me duele el estómago.
   (e) Me duelen los oídos.
   (f) Me duelen las axilas.
   (g) Me duelen los dedos.
   (h) Me duele la espalda.
   (i) Me duelen las rodillas.
   (j) Me duelen los pies.
   (k) Me duelen los intestinos.
4. (a) prescribió
   (b) indicó
   (c) informó
   (d) dio
   (e) prescribió
   (f) tomó
   (g) dio
   (h) informó
   (i) indicó

Role-Playing Exercise, Listening Comprehension Activity

   (a) sigo
   (b) con
   (c) miércoles
   (d) jueves
   (e) tobillo
   (f) izquierdos
   (g) Gracias
   (h) Hasta

Chapter 10
Dialog Comprehension

Su médico general le indicó al paciente hacer una cita con un médico nutricionista.
Mr. Mario Jiménez is consulting with a female nutritionist, (doctora).
The patient's diagnosis is overweight, hypertension, and high cholesterol.
The expression **tengo hambre** means I am hungry.
When the patient says **Como dos o tres porciones,** he is saying "I eat two or three servings."
The doctor does not give the patient any medication to help control his appetite. The patient will be checked again in two weeks.

Written Exercises

1. (a) Usted debería evitar las comidas altas en grasas.
   (b) Usted no debe fumar.
   (c) Usted debería evitar las comidas fritas.
   (d) Usted tiene que seguir una dieta.
   (e) Usted debe evitar el alcohol.
2. (a) En el consultorio del nutricionista
   Dialog order: 1, 14, 7, 6, 13, 4, 2, 9, 8, 3, 10, 5, 12, 11, 15

Chapters 6 to 10 Self-Check Exercise

1. palpitaciones; obstetra; fruta; comida; sobrepeso; camilla; vesícula; salmón; análisis; leche
2. (a) está
   (b) está
   (c) cuándo
   (d) Cuánto
   (e) tiene
3. (a) nutricionista
   (b) pediatra
   (c) médico general
   (d) cardiólogo
   (e) urólogo
   (f) 2
   (g) 5
   (h) 3
   (i) 8
4. (a) 6
   (b) 4
   (c) 1
   (d) 7
   (e) 9
5. (a) 2
   (b) 1
   (c) 4
   (d) 3
   (e) 5

Chapter 11
Dialog Comprehension

La Señora María Lares está en el consultorio del gastroenterólogo.
El Dr. Sánchez le indica un análisis de sangre, análisis de orina, una radiografía de estómago y una endoscopía.
El Dr. Sánchez le indica una dieta a María, y necesita los resultados de los estudios.

Written Exercises

1. (a) chicken pox, varicella
   (b) rubella
   (c) measles
   (d) mumps
   (e) smallpox
2. (a) ¿Fuma?
   (b) ¿Qué método anticonceptivo usa?
   (c) ¿Cuál es su peso habitual?
   (d) ¿Practica deportes?
   (e) ¿Ha tenido antecedentes de diabetes en su familia?
3. (a) Have you had veneral diseases?
   (b) ¿Ha sido hospitalizado?
   (c) ¿Ha tenido cirugías?
   (d) ¿Es alérgico a alguna medicina?
   (e) Have you (ever) been administered (given) general anesthesia?

Appendix 2, Verb References
Present Tense Exercises

-ar ending: (a) estudiamos; (b) cenan; (c) trabajas; (d) analiza; (e) hablo
-er ending: (a) come; (b) como; (c) lee; (d) bebe; (e) bebe
-ir ending: (a) insiste; (b) viven; (c) insistimos; (d) vive; (e) escribe

Past Tense, *ser* and *estar*

(a) estuvimos; (b) estuvo; (c) fue; (d) fue; (e) estuvo

Past Tense Regular Verbs, *-ar, -er, -ir* Endings

(a) asistió; (b) esperaron; (c) comió; (d) decidimos; (e) tomé

Past Tense Irregular Verbs

(a) fuimos; (b) dijo; (c) tuvo; (d) hiciste; (e) tuvo

Present Perfect

(a) ha indicado; (b) ha referido; (c) he seguido; (d) ha recomendado; (e) han comido.

Index

About the Author

Born in Buenos Aires, Argentina, Claudia Adjemian Kechkian has a degree in English from the *Pontificia Universidad Católica Argentina Santa María de los Buenos Aires*. She served at the same university as an Assistant Professor of English Grammar and was an Assistant and an Adjunct Professor of English Grammar at the *Universidad del Salvador*, also in Buenos Aires. Professor Kechkian has been teaching English and Spanish as a second and foreign language for twenty years in Argentina and the United States. She also has been a Medical Spanish instructor at the Physician Assistant Program at Barry University School of Graduate Medical Sciences, Miami Shores, Florida.

Professor Kechkian strongly believes in the power of good communication and open attitudes. To encourage the learning of a language, she emphasizes what she has observed in doctor/patient exchanges and other situations: that the power of a good relationship goes beyond native fluency in a language. She affirms that the better a person can handle a language, the more chances there will be for a more fluent communication. Nevertheless, a few words said with an open, kind, and professional attitude at the appropriate time are endlessly more effective than a language spoken with native fluency but without the same sensitivity to the situation.

Born in a family of Armenian origin, Professor Kechkian recalls how kindly and professionally their Spanish-speaking family physician used to sit next to her Armenian-speaking grandmother, as both made efforts to communicate with each other. Each gesture, word, and movement counted, but above all, what really counted were their attitudes, open and ready to understand each other, no matter who else was there serving as a translator.

CD Track Numbers